# SUPERNATURAL POWER
## *of the* BELIEVER

The Secrets To Growing In The Five
Dimensions Of God's Power

**By**
**UEBERT ANGEL, Ph.D**

*Spirit*Library
PUBLICATIONS

Spirit Library Publications
Manchester
UNITED KINGDOM


SUPERNATURAL Power of the Believer
Secrets To Growing In The Five Dimensions Of
God's Power
ISBN 978-0-955 8116-9-2

Unless otherwise stated, all scripture quotations
are taken from the King James Version of the
Bible.


Copyright 2010 by Uebert Angel


Published by Spirit Library Publications,
Manchester U.K.

Printed in the United Kingdom of Great Britain. All rights
reserved under International Copyright law. Contents and or
cover may not be reproduced in whole or in part in any form
without the express written consent of the publisher.

# CONTENTS

# CHAPTER ONE

## A Believer: The New Superman!

**Therefore if any man be in Christ, he is a NEW CREATURE: old things are passed away; Behold, all things are become knew (2 Cor. 5 vs. 17)**

**KAINOS** is the Greek word for *new creature*. This word means an UNHEARD OF creature, a new species of being, *unworn* and *utterly unique*. Kainos is a creature that never existed before. This new creature is superior to the devil and his gang and has an ability to grow in their super human qualities. Believers can move into higher realms of Power in Christ. They are born to demonstrate power. We are born to show the world that there is another world other than this physical one. We are born to perform miracles, signs and wonders.

The word says:

**'For the Kingdom of God is not in word, but in the demonstration of power' (1 Corinthians 4:20).**

Notice, as new creatures in Christ we are created to do mighty works and we can move high up in our dimensions of power. God made us to be so. We are God's products carrying His D.N.A.

James also says *'we are the workmanship (tecknon) of God'* meaning, the technology of God- His workmanship. We are God's make, packaged for success and victory. Believers are the new species. We are the new and best products on the market. We are the new superman born of God. We can do mighty exploits if we know how to move in the dimensions of God's power and in this book I will show you clearly how to do just that. After you get a hold of this revelation the devil and his gang will tremble at the mere sight of you.

We are able to grow because we are God's real sperm. It might shock some to hear this but if you follow the word of God closely you will be amazed at the claims of God over our lives as believers.

Just look at this...

**"...being born again, not of corruptible seed, but of incorruptible** →) God's sperm **Seed..." (1 Peter 1 vs. 23)**

Now, the word *seed* there is SPERMA in Greek meaning *sperm. So* SPERMA is where the English language took the word **sperm**. Do you see that according to the word of God we are actually God's sperm. His 'SPERMA,' powered by God's very own cells and DNA. We are big. We have Christ in us and we can increase in size with regards to power!

Remember Christ said;

**"...I am with you always, even unto the end of the world".**
**Matthew 28 vs. 20b**

If Christ is in us as believers, being God's actual sperm, we are GOD CARRIERS. We carry God around. It is absolutely simple. We have God in us. The KAINOS has God in them. This is the level of life that only believers possess; no one else can have this except us.

We are the UNHEARD OF creatures, a new species of

being, *unworn* and *utterly unique*. We are new on the scene. We are the new kind of species on the block. We never existed before. We are Superior to the devil and his gang. See!

*[handwritten: — Dunamis — Ischus — epikaizo]*

## The Power

This power is in five *dimensions*; the *kratos*, the *dunamis*, the *Ischus*, the *exousia* and the *epikaizo* dimension. The church has been used to only two, the dunamis dimension and the exousia dimension yet there are other dimensions that if a believer gets a hold of, they would shock their world with power and win sinners to the love of Christ. With this soul winning would be easy.

We have a power so big that when Apostle Paul got a hold of it, handkerchiefs that he touched rubbed off of that anointing and started healing the sick. Some people even brought aprons which he in turn touched and they became healing aprons.

Apostle Paul got a hold of this power to the extent that he proclaimed some controversial statements. He said;

**If the spirit of him that raised Christ from the dead dwells**
**inside of you, He that raised Christ from the dead shall**
**vitalise your mortal body by His Spirit that dwells in you.**
**Romans 8 vs. 11**

IN the believer is a power potential that will cause a lot of signs, miracles, and wonders to happen. Real exploits will happen when the believer grows in the five dimensions of God. It is mind blowing!

As for the Apostle Peter, his very shadow healed sick folk. Many sick folk were brought in the streets as he passed by; and when the shadow of Apostle Peter touched them, they got healed of all their diseases. That was a demonstration of the power we have as believers. The KAINOS which we are possess this power. We have this power in us. We have this ability. **We are the new superman in Christ. We control our situations.**

As aforementioned, you will learn how to increase in the anointing through growing in the five dimensions of God's power.

In fact, believers are the only race of people tattooed by name in the palms of God.

**"Behold, I have graven (tattooed) thee upon the palms of my hands..."**
**Isaiah 49 vs. 16**

The finger prints of God run all over us with a mighty surge of supernatural power that makes miracles (be it financial, spiritual, or physical), an everyday occurrence and sends diseases packing.

We are the new supermen. You and I are by the grace of God endowed with the right to become children of God. We are His technology, His make, His produce, His seed!

Understand this is a right and not a privilege. Though we can grow into obedient children, we do not grow into sons and daughters of God because the moment we believe, we become sons, just as your child becomes your child the moment he/she is conceived. They don't have to wait until they are old for them to be your children, they just become, because you gave birth to them.

The Lord Jesus says *the son does what he sees the father do.* Now, what does the father do? He is creative, He heals the sick, in Him there is no guile, no sin can be found in Him, He is the owner of everything seen or unseen, He performs the impossible, to Him anything is possible, He performs miracles...AND SO MUST THE SONS, *for the son does what he sees the father do.*

## I AM More Than A Handkerchief!

You are more than what you think you are. In you resides a power so strong and mighty that after you get a hold of this revelation the devil and his gang will tremble at the mere sight of you.

Notice, if Paul's handkerchief was handed to people and they would get healed - how much more you who are called to be partakers of God's OWN SPERMA. If aprons were taken from Paul and those aprons would carry an anointing to raise the dead, destroy cancer - how much more you who are called to be partakers of God's divine nature. You are more than an apron! You carry God around and miracles can't help themselves but show up. You are more than Paul's handkerchief. You are God's very own make. You are endowed with supernatural power!

However, there are five DIMENSIONS of power that we ought to move into and realise there is a way to go.

## The Five Dimensions Of God's Power

When Apostle Paul writes to churches, he uses five words to describe power and many translations of the bible have unfortunately interchangeably used them. These Greek words are very different and not only are they distinct, they carry a dimensional difference, meaning to say; these are levels of power rather than just words.

One believer might only be in one level and in that they

show power that goes hand in hand with that level. See, power can be measured. The anointing can be measured. It can be calculated and differs in levels.

Notice here,

**'...Christ given the Spirit without measure.'**
**John 3 vs. 34**

If Christ's anointing had no measure, then, that shows that some are in a measure. This is the same with power, it can be measured and some believers might possess more power than others. This is why we have some believers who can do more exploits in the Lord than others. Some do not even show any sign of power, and worse still, some are unaware of any power.

This secret is inside the revelation the Apostle Paul received. In it one will see that there are dimensions one can move up to on the ladder to the highest level of power in God. Now, this is not a natural movement, it is a spiritual movement and since in the spirit time does not exist, that means any believer can attain the highest level of power in a short time on a natural timescale.

A believer with the revelation of these five dimensions of power and how each one works will be the one to be used mightily in signs, miracles and wonders. They will experience the supernatural in their lives and in other people's lives, in day to day living as touching their own surroundings, bodies, finances and every other aspect of life. See, there are higher levels of life, greater power zones where anything is very possible.

Look at Joshua. On the day the Lord gave the Israelites victory over the Amorites, Joshua prayed to the Lord in front of all the people of Israel. He said,

**"Let the sun stand still over Gibeon, and the moon**

over the valley of Aijalon". So the sun and moon stood still until the Israelites had defeated their enemies.
Joshua 10 vs. 12-13 (NLT)

You see how he stopped the sun and stopped the moon and even told them where to stop, and the moon as well as the sun obeyed the words of a man. If you see how the writer continues to tell us what that meant. He says;

"The Lord fought for Israel that day. Never before or since has there been a day like that one, when the Lord answered such a request from a human being".
Joshua 10 vs. 14 (NLT)

Did you see that? It says there is no man before that or after that who God listened to in that manner. How can that be?

Look again at Samuel how the word did not say he was just a mere Prophet, hearing and reporting. The word says if Samuel said something, God would listen to it just like what happened to Joshua. In fact, Samuel was a different breed of believer in the Old Testament. The man's words were so loaded and dangerous that if he would think something and say it, God would avail Himself to obey the words of Samuel. God allowed it and gave him that authority that he would speak and God would perform. That is why the bible says,

"No word of Samuel was put to the ground..."
1 Samuel 3 vs. 19

Samuel's every word would be done by the Lord. Not even a word was put to the ground. Samuel spoke and God performed. It was all because of his dimension of power in the Lord. His dimension had gotten too big to play with! He had touched the invincibility of God's power. He was now a dangerous man for the devil to mess with.

May I also remind you of Moses who had to be reminded to die by the Lord. See it for yourself again.

**"Go unto Mount Nebo... and die"**
**Deuteronomy 32 vs. 49,50**

The man was going to continue living if God had not come to remind him. This is because of his dimension in the Lord's power. He had touched a greater dimension than others for him to live such a life.

The Lord Jesus walked on water, cast out demons with ease, cursed trees and they withered. The Lord could speak to trees and trees would hear. He had the Spirit without measure. His anointing was too high and His dimension too big. It was just off the charts!

### The Words for Power

Notice how Apostle Paul uses these words in one verse.

**"And what is the exceeding greatness of his power (***dunamis***) in us who believe, according to the working (***energy***) of his mighty power (***ischus kratos***)" Ephesians 1:19**

Someone might say, "I don't care about these words". Yet how do you expect to know what Paul said if you don't know what he meant. If Apostle Paul plays around with all these words, we cannot just ignore them and say they do not matter. If they mattered to Apostle Paul they should matter to us. AND boy, they do matter!

Three words appear there with exception of ***exousia***

which means authority. The English translation of the bible gives no right credit to these words. They carry so much revelation that they should not have been left that way. This confusion has caused most Christians to only have an acquaintance with two words of power which are **dunamis** and **exousia,** yet having an awareness of only these will not do much for the believer.

_Exousia_ is translated _authority,_ and _dunamis_ is the _God given ability to effect a change._ These two can look very powerful, yet they do not bring the maximum power God intends us to have.

Now, someone might say "all I need is dunamis and exousia that's all," but they would be deceived since the word says this dunamis works hand in hand with other higher levels and greater degrees of power. Without that higher dimension properly stationed, dunamis will not cause or effect a great change in someone's life or in any situation given. Dunamis will not do much if not in line with greater dimensions of power. You see, this is a revelation that is easy to understand but very difficult to catch if you already think you know. Remember the word says;

**"If the light that is in you be darkness, you are in great Darkness".**
**Matthew 6vs. 23**

If you think you know much already, you will not benefit from greater revelations in the word of God that He wants you to know. You see, it is very difficult, in fact impossible to fill up a cup that is already full. There is just no space to pour anything else.

### Dunamis works with other dimensions

*God given ability to effect a change*

Dunamis has to be connected to a greater level of power for it to flow from within you. Notice this verse again;

**"and what is the immeasurable greatness of His** *dunamis* **in us who believe according to His** *energes* **of His** *ischus kratos"*

Notice, Apostle Paul said the *dunamis* power in us works **ACCORDING** to the energy of *ischus kratos. Dunamis* works according to the level which you are in and if you do not know about the ischus kratos how do you expect to do what the Lord said;     *his mighty power*

**"...Greater signs than these shall ye do..."**
**John 14 vs.12**

This is why some Christians attack and persecute those who are demonstrating the power of God. They are accustomed to lower dimensions of power to the extent that they cannot accept anyone being used in a unique way.

I remember a time when I drove my brother's new Nissan, it was a joy to drive with all the comfort and the automatic gearbox. I enjoyed the ride a lot that I thought at that time there was no better make than that. It had all the things a car should have, or so I thought. I got so caught up in the beauty of the Nissan that when I got into a new Mercedes E- Class, I truly got confused. This was now a new world. The car could read speed limits all by itself. It could see when I was going off the road. It controlled its own speed and had a lot of things inside that when you drive it without learning it, you may think it was malfunctioning. Well it wasn't malfunctioning, I was the one malfunctioning.

I was the one who was used to malfunctioning. I was used to the Nissan that the Mercedes E- class' functionality seemed like it was a malfunction. I could no longer drive my Mercedes like I was in a Nissan. I had to learn the ways of the Mercedes for it had higher levels of class

*[Handwritten annotations at top:]*

*Exousia — Authority*

*Devil got no power got from Adam*

*Ex: In a Football Referey have exousia*
*Players — Dunamis*

and gizmos that needed my attention.

This is exactly like the power dimensions. If you are in one dimension, you will think there should be some deliverance you need to take place in your life, when you actually do not need deliverance. You need a revelation, an apocalypses, an opening that will cause light to enter into your system concerning these dimensions of power so that your life will change to a higher realm of spirituality.

*[Handwritten: A Authority.]*

There are higher realms of power which believers need to know. There is **dunamis,** and then **dunamis** has to be coupled with **exousia,** which will have to work with **kratos.** Dunamis alone is not enough. It is the inherent power and needs other realms to make it very strong. One needs some **kratos** for the equation to begin to work and also we have **ischus and epikaizo** for all the dimensions to be in place.

*[Handwritten: God given ability to effect a change]*

In this book, you will discover that for you to paralyze the devil, you would need a lot of **kratos,** (besides epikaizo), more than you use all the other dimensions of power. So we have *kratos, epikaizo, ischus, exousia,* and *dunamis* to work with. I will explain each of them in detail. These are dimensions which the Spirit of the Lord has opened to me to teach in this book, so that whosoever receives this revelation, will move with so much power that the devil and his cohorts will shake at the mere sight of you. This revelation will make you invincible.

See, *dunamis (power to effect a change)* is the main word for power most Christians know. *Exousia,* which generally means authority, is also known in many Christian quarters, especially charismatic circles and evangelical circles. The deep meaning of these same words through the Spirit of God will be taught here in the pages of this book till you begin to grasp what the Lord wants you to move in.

I know that these dimensions that are higher are hidden to many and how to grow in them is little known and rarely taught.

## Further Introduction To The dimensions

After *dunamis* and *exousia,* we find some very important words; *ischus* and *kratos.* These are some very important words penned by the Apostle Paul showing us other dimensions of power. In them we see that believers, if taught well, can do extraordinary exploits that will shock this world.

I have personally touched this power in my life. I have touched the power many times where the Lord, by revelation on these words has caused me to experience the prophetic, where I tell people events that have happened in their lives and call out their names without prior knowledge of their existence. I know when future events will happen with clarity. I have also experienced supernatural transportation, where I am in one place this moment and in another the next. I am talking about a seven mile distance, travelling to places physically in seconds with no jet, not even using a car.

Angels have appeared around the pulpit many times as I preached and some people in the church saw them. This is the life we are talking about. A life that will 'raise' your enemies' eyebrows. A life that will shake your world for Christ. A life that troubles your enemy, at the same time getting them to think.

At one time I was in the city centre of Manchester after shopping with my wife. We got into the car and before putting the key into the ignition, we found ourselves seven miles away, parked in front of our house. That's travelling at a fraction of a second. I have seen the blind healed and the lame walk in crusades we hold around the world. At one time the Lord made me walk through a wall. I literally walked out of a room which was fully locked. The Lord has granted us extraordinary miracles through his *ischus kratos*. He has shown us a lot of things. (His mighty power)

One day I was teaching on this subject in church, in broad daylight, in Manchester, when I was raised by the Holy Spirit centimetres above the ground in front of people. I levitated in the air to the utter amazement of not only myself but those who were present. This is due to this revelation you are holding, and it's not something you can force people to understand or to believe; you just know on your own that this is it. It is the *kratos* of God. It is a higher dimension in God. It is a *kratos* dimension far above the normal power adds power to the inherent one which is dunamis.

This is not for everyone. This revelation is only for those who want to surprise their world. It is a revelation of ultimate victory and the intertwining of these dimensions produce such an ability that guarantees a life of victory in a believer and forms a force that will permeate our natural life.

In this book are all the dimensions as God instructed me to write them and how to increase in each dimension to the extent where miracles become an everyday occurrence in your life.

## CHAPTER TWO

## Kratos And Epikaizo Dimension

### KRATOS

At this dimension, demons shake, serpents are trodden underfoot, and diseases are sent packing. *Kratos* is a level of invincibility. This is the level of immunity to all possibilities of failure, defeat, poverty, and hurt is disarmed. It is a level that is destruction proof. The *kratos* level is a stage of invincibility. It is a power dimension that renders the devil and his cohorts useless. It sterilises the demons of hell. In short, this is the power level of absolute victory, just behind EPIKAIZO.

This is the level the Lord meant when He uttered the famous words that;

**"...you shall tread upon serpents and scorpions and they shall by no means hurt you..."**
**Luke 10 vs.19**

In the book of Mark He said;

**"Those who believe (follow instruction) they shall lay hands on the sick and they shall be healed... if they drink any deadly thing it will not hurt them..."**
**Mark 16 vs. 17,18**

Notice, the power the Lord has given us is too enormous. You would think it's all fantasy, if this *kratos* is not stationed well in your spirit. This is too much power!

## The power of labelling

The power we can have under kratos ability if not understood can get people to see every man or woman of God who does exploits to be doing it by some dark force from the dark world. All this is called the demon of labelling. The devil realised that if he says ministers who do miracles are fake it might not hold water so he decided to label God's power as his own. What he did was to claim everything done as his own so believers would stay blinded to his devices.

The dimensions in this book can make a mere human to be superhuman and will cause immature Christians to not understand how things are being done. Remember in the times of the Lord here on earth.

The book of John 7 vs. 12 says;

**"...Some said he is a good man and yet some said for sure He deceiveth people..."**

This was the Lord Himself. In fact some of his own family said he was mad and the priests said the demons were to blame. Do you see that? When power comes on you there is the devil also on the sidelines to confuse believers so they will not get the truth.

## Back to Kratos

Kratos will appear too good to be true, if you have no real revelation concerning these power dimensions and how to mature in them. The word of the Lord in both books of Mark and Luke shows clearly the power of invincibility. They show the great immunity one possesses with *kratos* power. Serpents, scorpions, poison, and deadly disease are not able to touch you. That can only be the *kratos* power level. The level of invincibility and immunity!

Look at what the Apostle Paul says about this level;

**"And what is the exceeding greatness of his dunamis (power) to us-ward who believe, ACCORDING to the energes (working) of his ischus (mighty) *kratos* (power)" (Ephesians 1:19)**

Here he says something that God proclaimed to me and said "son how do you expect to grow when you do not care what Paul said". I could not understand what the Lord meant until He clearly opened it up to me. There is **dunamis**, then there is **ischus**, there is **energes**, there is also **kratos**. He said go to **kratos**, and He called it the level of immunity.

## The Immunity And Invincibility

I remember when I became a believer, and went into full time ministry I learnt a lot about demonic power. You see, as a young believer all I learnt then was about God's anger and the power of demons to kill and maim believers. Every prayer that was done was done to counteract the power of demons. I got so frightened about the whole thing that everything became the devil, including the company that made the cleaning detergents in the house. I would listen to anything the pastor was saying about the devil and from there I formed my own understanding, a mindset, a phronesis, that the devil was so powerful he would even kill me at the speed of thought. I got so scared. That was the absence of *kratos* consciousness.

I did not know I could be immune and invincible. I just thought the devil was just out to get me, and there was nothing I could do but dive and duck; but when I allowed God to start working in my soul about the dimensions of power and the *kratos* power, something lit up in my spirit like a neon bulb. Just like that, I got to understand the dimension of absolute victory and success. I began to see myself as a success and demons started to check out as fast as I got onto the pulpit.

In my crusades, I have seen demons trying to attack me but nothing happens. They all end up leaving. They can now sense the *kratos* of God in me; the force of God inside me. This is the level of diplomatic immunity!

In Ephesians 6.10, Apostle Paul, after writing a power packed letter to the Ephesians church, gives a conclusion that sums up everything here. He says;

**"Finally my brethren be *"dunamo"* (strong) in the Lord and in the *KRATOS (power)* of his *ischus (might)"***

The Apostle was back with the word *kratos,* and putting it as a conclusion, shows he meant it; and that concurs with how the Lord told me to keep it in my spirit and teach the church this dimension, and how to grow in it.

### The Uniqueness Of Kratos Power

*Kratos* refers to the engine of control. It is the power behind control; it is the power of invincibility; it drives the facility of control.

For example, when a lion wants to bite you, you release *kratos* power that created it and shut its mouth. That is *kratos* ability; its available to every believer. Daniel, a man who was not even born again, used it at its boiling point;

**"Daniel who by faith shut the mouth of the lions..."**
**Hebrews 11 vs. 33**

His faith was too high up in another degree of power that could work wonders. It could shut the lion's mouth and using another dimension could even tame its anger in the flash of a second. Daniel was an Old Testament believer. He was not born again, yet he got a revelation that moved him to greater levels in the **kratos** dimension of power. When he coupled KRATOS and EPIKAIZO - It was so much that the lions lost appetite when he stepped into their den.

The book of Daniel chapter six says he was not found with even the slightest hurt or harm because;

"...he believed in his God..."
**Daniel 6 vs. 23**

This believing is different because the word is clear;

**"...be it prophecy let it be done according to the level of faith" Romans 12 vs. 6**

This is indicative to the fact that whatever Daniel could have said to get out, all was dependant on his faith in the Lord. ***"Be it prophecy let it be done to the measure of faith"***. This faith is of a higher level in the kratos dimension. The power and engine of control that is able to tame lions and adding EPIKAIZO could make them lose appetite. *Kratos power controls everything. It is the level of force*!

This is the power that works in us and the strength of it in us determines how we can reach it.

Joshua went back behind the authority of the sun and the moon to the engine that controlled them and he controlled their normal behaviour. He even moved them around and told them where to stop by name and they obeyed. No argument! They did not offer resistance. You never heard of anything in the Bible where the moon said

"I do not feel like doing that!", or the sun say to Joshua, "I don't want to go where you are telling me to go, it's too far" or "it's not my usual way of doing things".

The *kratos* in these men caused high natural laws to bend and follow another reality those elements had never followed before. They caused animals to obey, and to be tamed. They walked on water opposing the molecular density of water. These men and women were opposing the natural laws. They were using another law from another realm. The realm of the supernatural was so real to them they could access it anytime. These men did not question anything. To them, their reality was the only reality that could be followed. The *kratos* power was so big and stationed in them so much so they surprised their world and caused many to marvel at the mighty power that they demonstrated.

The *kratos* level causes natural laws to bend for its concentration is in the spiritual realm.

### Ephesians 1 vs. 19b, 20a
### "...according to the working of his great *kratos* which he energised in Christ"

You see what Ephesians 1vs. 19b says about *kratos* being centred in the very being of Christ, the anointed and his anointing. This is where it's centred. It is the centre of creation and controls all creation. This is the power of the word!

*Kratos* is the power of the **Word** and the Word is the Lord Jesus Christ. It is the place which makes all the other dimensions of power exist. This is its greatest uniqueness. *Kratos* is there so that *dunamis, ischus, and exousia* can function properly. Without it, nothing really works as it is supposed to work.

This *kratos* is very unique. When you fellowship with

people with *kratos,* you see a higher glory even in their countenance. When you see those with *ischus,* you see a beautiful but different glory and that is the same with people with *dunamis* and those with *exousia.* However, the story changes when you meet giants in the faith that have managed to intertwine all the dimensions of power! That is a whole different breed. These people ooze power everywhere they are. They exude power and maturity in the spirit. In fact, you will just know when you get around them. It is explosive to be in their presence.

They are Jesus copies. They can literally walk on water and do mighty works. These people might not get the limelight, but they are there. Apart from myself being used in some of these exploits, I have seen many and still know many today that are used in ways that will shock the world. When they get the limelight, they are constantly persecuted. Some are called fakes, some, deceivers. Some are called swindlers, yet they are just there to do God's will. They did it to the Lord Jesus Himself. Check this;

**"some say (The Lord Jesus) was a good man
Some say nay he DECEIVES people" John 7 vs. 12**

Do you see that? The people thought the Lord Jesus was a CONMAN, they were not saying he was just using dark powers, they said he was a deceiver and a conman. His family said he was mentally disturbed.

**"the lad is beside himself" Mark 3 vs. 21**

The church and the preachers of his day blamed the devil for his way of doing things, for his miracles, his signs and wonders. They said the demons were at work and were to be blamed.

"He uses belzebub- king of demons to work mighty

works". Do you see that when these dimensions are stationed well in you many will think you are using dark forces? Far be it from immature people to ever think God is at work. ANY miracle of the Lord done by people with great power is always relegated to the devil. It is a shame.

## The Power Behind Creation

The Lord Jesus had the power of invincibility. The bible says he had the spirit with no measure. He possessed the anointing without measure.

**"Jesus ...given the Spirit without measure..." (John 3:34)**

The level of invincibility caused him to be a demolisher of all natural laws. He could oppose them at will. At times he could disappear. Just vanish into thin air. At times the Lord would just stand there and his attackers would not do anything to Him. Other times he would speak to inanimate objects and the objects would obey like they could speak and hear. He had a revelation of another realm of all possibility. He had *kratos* ability. He possessed invincibility. He was fully loaded with the power of immunity and all the other dimensions, plus more.

The Lord at other times opposed the law of viscosity. He opposed the molecular density of water. One day after He had let his disciples go to the other side of the body of water before him, He decided to follow them, the bible says He chose to go into another dimension and walked on water like it was solid concrete. See it here;

**"...he went to them walking on water..." Matthew 14:25**

Some versions say:

**"...He was there alone..." Matthew 14:23**

Indicating there was no one there including boats or boat operators.

Wow! He looked for the boat then decided, "Well I can just walk on the water, and I don't need a boat after all". That is the *kratos* power, the power that brought immunity from sinking. The power brought invincibility. Laws that have to do with water did not count. The laws that govern it had to bend because *kratos* goes behind the power of water and its laws. *Kratos* controls the engine. It is the engine of control that binds creation and renders all other natural laws useless and powerless.

At one time people wanted to throw the Lord down a cliff but the bible says he just turned and walked among them as He went His way. How? **Luke 4 vs. 30**

**"But He passing through the midst of them went his way". Luke 4:30**

Jesus literally disappeared. Their eyes were closed with something at the peak of *kratos* which we shall discuss later. Their eyes were so overshadowed that they could not see anything as he passed right in the middle of them. That's power, but still not all of it!

You see, some people think they already have the extreme grade of power, yet that would be a deception. See, If God is to manifest all his power today, we will all die and the rocks and mountains would explode and melt. That is why his appearance during the rapture will make people disappear, yet still that will not be his full power.

## The Highest Level Of Power Possible

*Kratos* itself is just the introduction of the highest power as aforementioned. It is higher than other dimensions, but has to work with these dimensions in order for it to function well.

## EPIKAIZO

**Epikaizo** is the boiling point of power, nearest to eternity. The more one stays in it, the more they are ready to step into glory, like Enoch and Elijah.

Many Christians think **Acts 1 vs. 8** which says, "…but ye shall receive power when the Holy Spirit has come upon you," is the highest level of power one can get. Well, that is just the beginning of power. There is still another realm of power, which is greater. This is the shadow of God. I know this might not be something many believers have heard, yet this is the reality of God.

**Epikaizo** is in the shadow of the Almighty. This is the power that came upon Mary to conceive. The bible says;

**"Then Mary said unto the angel, how shall this be, seeing I know not a man? And the angel answered and said unto her, the Holy Spirit shall come upon thee, and *the power of the Highest* shall *overshadow* thee…" (Luke 1:34-35)**

'Overshadow' is the word *epikaizo*, which has been used only three times in the New Testament. Look, it does not just say, "the power of the Holy Spirit" it says, "the power of the highest". That's where *kratos* power from the Spirit of God moves around. This is the highest possible power. This is the most extreme of the grade. It is the extravagant power. It is power poured out to the extent of gushing out to cause a change. It is *kratos* ability yet this is the end of the grade but higher than this is the overshadow level. **Kratos** moves into the overshadow level when it's fully placed. This is the boiling point of *kratos* Dimension and it's called 'epikaizo'.

Elijah and Enoch's *kratos* reached the highest level that they stepped into heaven in their physical bodies. They touched the very top end of *kratos* that they entered into the 'overshadow', the **epikaizo** stage and got lost into the glory. This was something too extreme that they were no longer able to live among mortals. *Humans at this level would not have been able to stand them. They were now too explosive for our* level.

### The *Kratos* And *Epikaizo* Dimensions

Look at what happened here in **Luke 9vs.29–35**. In verse 20 at the mountain of transfiguration it says;

**"As he prayed, the appearance of His face was altered, and his robe became white and glistering".**

This was the beginning; it altered his face and even his clothes. In the Old Testament Moses got a taste of this power that his face also changed and glistened, but it only ended there and his clothes did not glisten. The level of his ability or *kratos* was lower than that of the Lord Jesus Christ. The Lord Jesus Christ's clothes were changed just as his face was changed. That was tremendous power, but still it had not reached the *epikaizo*.

However, when you look further in verse 30-31 you hear that;

**"Elijah and Moses appeared in glory and spoke of Jesus' death..."**

You see, here Elijah and Moses and the Lord were discussing the *epikaizo;* that the Lord Jesus was to go through resurrection, and how best to talk about it than to try some of it right here. How good it is that they even spoke of this in the glory and went past the beginnings of *kratos* to its highest form of manifestation, the *epikaizo.* See this transition for yourself here in verse 32.

**"Meanwhile, Peter and those with him were heavy with sleep; When they were fully awake, they saw His glory and the two men that stood with him" Luke 9 vs. 32**

This was another dimension. The word said the disciples were "heavy with sleep and when they were fully awake..." What is this? It means more than you may think. It meant their senses of the spiritual were also awake just as their bodies were also awake and they saw this happening. An open vision was happening here. See!

They had been moved to another realm of power which was too dangerous but still not the highest form. This was powerful but not as powerful as the Lord they were about to experience or taste from afar as it were. This other dimension was the level where eternity touches the natural and breaks its laws. Kratos removes or opposes natural laws, whereby Epikaizo breaks and completely annihilates them.

In verse 35, the Lord God himself spoke and uttered;

**"This is my beloved son hear him"**

The beginning of this verse says;

**"A voice came out of the cloud"**

This was the **epikaizo**. It was an overshadowing voice.

That is why one verse **(Verse 34)** before this you read:

"**...while he was saying this, a cloud came and** *overshadowed* **them.**"

*Epikaizo* was now in progress. It overshadowed and offered a blockage; it broke laws of nature. Even the highest of the laws of nature and rendered them powerless. It controlled them to the extent that the natural could not be seen.

You see, *Epikaizo* means to block something from view. This means this highest level of *kratos* breaks all natural laws from operating. It removes or blocks them from operating. It goes beyond opposing natural laws. Even the force of gravity will not touch it, that's why Elijah went up with no resistance from the force of gravity. That is why Enoch did the same. In fact, this is why I was given grace once in my life to levitate opposing the very law of gravity. I had received a level where this law would not touch me, but I had not touched it consistently like these men did.

Notice what happened to the disciples here. Peter started acting like a crazy man. He spoke of building tents and the Bible proves he was now confused by this level of power. See this;

**"He said this for lack of things to say" Luke 9:33**

The power was too much that he did not know what to say anymore, it was more than he bargained for. In fact, as they spoke of this nonsense of building tents, they were overshadowed. They were '*epikaizoed*' and immediately their view was blocked.

**"...they could not see anything but the cloud..."**

Epikaizo was happening. Kratos had gone to its extreme that epikaizo blocked the natural laws and their sight could not be used to see the supernatural. At this level, open vision can be blocked and the sight of many seers becomes blurred. The disciples had reached a level next to heaven's volts.

They could not see anymore. If they had been permitted to see through, their eyes would have exploded.

However, *epikaizo* can work behind the scenes in healing because it is the top end of the highest level of *kratos* and works by transforming natural cells into supernatural cells. It works in a measure and is released in a measure but even its smallest measure is too powerful. That is why Peter could use it. Notice Peter's *epikaizo* on people!

**"At least the shadow of Peter passing by might fall on them" Acts 5:15**

Peter's shadow healed the sick because it overshadowed the sick people's mortal bodies. That was Peter's level of *epikaizo*, not the raw *epikaizo* of God. This *epikaizo* Peter used performed a lot of miracles and not only miracles, but extraordinary miracles. These were great miracles that had not been seen in that place before. *Epikaizo* appeared and blocked natural laws and diseases were sent packing.

You see, under *epikaizo*, diseases are nothing, demons don't trouble you, chaos cannot stand, nothing bad can exist, and poverty cannot exist. It is a level of the highest power possible.

## Creative Miracles

This level is very gigantic indeed. When you talk of creative miracles you will be talking about *epikaizo*.

I remember, in the Caribbean Islands, when I was at a crusade where thousands upon thousands were in attendance including heads of different states. Here we had five people with a limb shorter than the other. Four had short legs and one had a short arm. Here, I am not talking millimetres of difference in length; I am talking of many centimetres difference. All grew in front of the people who were present.

My spiritual father, Kenneth Hagin, was used extremely in this end of *kratos*. He was used in the *epikaizo* level. There is also Prophet Victor Boateng, a man God gave me to be mentored by when papa Kenneth Hagin passed away and this man's epikaizo is seen mainly in the prophetic. Whilst I am at this point, i believe a person should have one spiritual father. However what God did with me was to give me a father that would get me somewhere and when he left this world God had already told me that Prophet Victor Boateng would be my father and that is what took place. All this I received in a vision from the Lord. So in that there are two men that have made deposits in my life and continue to do so and that is Prophet Kenneth Hagin and Prophet Victor Boateng. His level of the prophetic is so high one would not find words when they see it in its prime. Prophet Victor Boateng has been used in miracles through the prophetic that when you see it happen you can be convinced that dimensions exist.

These miracles carry a different height than the normal ones. This is when *kratos* works by intertwining *ischus, dunamis* and *exousia* to the maximum level that you start oozing with this combination. You see, *epikaizo* is the highest end of *kratos* that has been stationed in you by combining all the dimensions of power. It is the top end of power that will astonish the devil and his cohorts. It destroys his focus very easily. *Kratos* is power of invincibility grown by utilising all the other levels of power through the word and prayer. *Epikaizo* is the highest grade of power. It is power that is next to the volts of heaven. It is a fearsome power.

Notice at the transfiguration, the disciples were not afraid of Moses or Elijah. They even wanted to make tents for them because the level of power had not reached *epikaizo*. It was just *kratos* on its way to the top which is *epikaizo*, the overshadowing.

However, when the *epikaizo* came, you hear the words;

**"...they were all afraid..."** (Luke 9:34)

It brings fear. This is why men and women of God who walk in this power are not easy to be around. They radiate with so much power you think they are not human.

Here, I am not talking about the celebrity conscious world that has turned preachers into vain celebrities. No way, that is not what I am referring to. I am talking about serious power emissions coming out of these people that it's even difficult to talk to them. They are too loaded with ability it will make you dizzy just being around them.

### *Epikaizo* Is Fearsome

I remember when I was taken to heaven in a vision and I experienced this epikaizo, the top end of kratos that has been stationed by using all levels of power and also by His grace. I was taken to where the Lord stood from His throne and He was standing facing His throne that my view was looking upon his back. I could see angels moving in and out around Him. His arms were stretched out and the glory around Him was so brilliant that music came out of His body. As He turned to face me, a force so strong hit me and threw me back into my body that I came out of the vision.

After I came out of this vision I tried to leave my bedroom, for it was now around ten in the morning. I tried to move towards my door but the glory was too much, yet it was still not full epikaizo. It was just the beginning of it. I had just experienced it. The world did not make any more sense. All the ornaments I was seeing in my bedroom looked like nothing in comparison to the epikaizo dimension I had just experienced. No matter how expensive and beautiful those ornaments were, they were put to nothing by that level of epikaizo.

Before I could gather or compose myself, the walls in my house disappeared out of sight. Epikaizo was growing now. The windows left and I saw the clouds from afar approaching at high speed towards the top floor of my house that had been transformed to clear ground. As they approached, I saw a light in them. The light started small but began to grow bigger and bigger until the Lord shown through them. The speed was so tremendous. It was faster than the speed of light. It looked faster than the speed of thought. I just knew it. It couldn't be slower than light and sound. It was fast!

When I saw the Lord in heaven, the glory was conceivable because my spirit was beholding Him and not my body, but this time, this was getting into my body and it looked like I would jump out of my flesh. My bones felt as if they could jump out of my muscles. The power was just unbearable. It was fearsome. I understood what happened to Daniel. He said...

**"I fell asleep as dead and retained no strength..."**
**Daniel 10:5-8**

John in the book of Revelation had the same experience.

He could not stand at all. The power was epikaizo. It overshadowed him to the extent that he fell as if dead.

When the Lord Jesus Christ came to where I stood shaking in my room that had been transformed, I tried to look at Him. I tried with all my might to see Him, but my blood seemed to boil within me; and the light around Him, I could not stand. The light looked like burning liquid light that was too hot to touch or to look at. I could not handle it. I rushed to where I knew the bed was but could not see my bed, and I instinctively pulled a duvet from my bed and covered myself. The fear of the Lord came over me to such an extent that I could not bear to look at the Lord Jesus Christ. This is not fear that makes you afraid but awe. His power was not only hot, but extremely untouchable. I could not look into his eyes and I blocked myself from the view or rather, his power moved my hands so that I could not get 'hurt' by the power. Awe came over me and that's what epikaizo, the highest creative power of God, can do. It overwhelms you. You begin to understand how powerful the Lord is, and it convicts you of sin.

This power, when you have it, people will fear and demons will fear. Many unfortunately will think that you have some kind of evil power. Remember, many thought the Lord was not only possessed, but called Him

**"...beelzebub..." Mark 3:22**

This means the father of demons. This was a higher level of power where people become jealous and try to destroy you by calling you names, and accusing you of being an evil possessor or a fake. They said Jesus was a fake too!

**"...he is a good man, yet some SAID NAY HE DECEIVETH PEOPLE" John 7:12.**

Jesus was accused of being a fake. The epikaizo became too big that the people said what Jesus did was not possible unless he was cheating somehow. They began to think what he did was too extreme that the only way was deception.

In the prophetic, we also find that power under the epikaizo, that it amazes people how I know people's history, present, and future. It boggles their minds how people's addresses, postal boxes, post codes, zip codes, mobile numbers and future events to the date they will happen, are known under the prophetic anointing. It boggles their minds. What they do not know is that there is an epikaizo dimension where you are too engrossed in the glory that all these details come rushing into your mouth and you utter them.

For example, epikaizo got a hold of me that I mentioned the death of Michael Jackson by the month, week, and date before it happened. I even described how he was going to be rushed to the hospital. I have seen too many things happening by date and time and this is where people cannot understand. They can't get the point that when epikaizo happens, it requires revelation to understand it and no argument.

How on earth do I tell the death of presidents or individuals by date? Do I phone those people, telling them when to die in the exact way they do? It is epikaizo! It confuses the immature!

We will talk about growing in epikaizo later on in this book. Before moving on, let's touch Kratos a little bit more.

### Back To Developing Kratos

Kratos is the power of the word – simple. The amount of word in you determines the amount of kratos power in you. You should be filled with enough word that when the pressures of life come, all that comes out of you is word juice.

37

Kratos is the realm of word. The word of God should be like the Prophet Jeremiah;

**"...It is like fire shut up in my bones..."**
**Jeremiah 20 vs.9**

The word should be soaked deep down within you. You have to spend countless hours in the word so that what comes out of you is simply the word. The word of God should spread like wildfire around your life. You should be too convinced of God's word that even if someone brings 29 versions of the bible plus a shotgun to try and move you from it, you will not believe them. You are solid on the word. That is the kratos level and you can start today.

Understand, the word says;

**"The entrance of the word giveth light"**
**Psalms 119 vs. 130**

The word 'light' here after 'the entrance of the word' is equivalent to the word '*photizo*' meaning stadium lights. This stadium light effect will happen in your spirit and will permeate your body to the level where even your shadow will be affected. See what Peter did,

**"the shadow of Peter could fall on them and heal them" (Acts 5:15)**

The shadow was possessed by God's word!

He had drunk from the cistern of God's word that the power that was a light in his spirit could be experienced even through a shadow. Do you see what the word can do? It can possess you.

Many believers eat three times a day, but feed their

spirits with one cold sandwich of the word per day. Their lives reflect that coldness. They can have some power, but not a lot of it. They can talk the word, but they are not strong enough to walk the word. To them, walking the word is not only difficult, but many times impossible even though they talk it. Kratos is the level of complete submission to the word, and when the word becomes submitted to, an overshadowing will take place. Epikaizo will take place. See what happened to Mary and what she said. See her response to the word;

**"let it be done to me as you have planned" (Luke 1:38)**

She submitted to the word fully until the epikaizo happened. An overshadowing suddenly took place when she submitted to God's word from the word of the angel Gabriel. It was this level of submission that turned kratos into epikaizo, the power next to eternity. Kratos dimension is word dimension. Spend hours daily in the word and see what happens.

## God Submits To His Word Too

See, God respects His word. In fact, the book of **Psalms 138 vs. 2** says...

**"He has exalted His name above all names and His word above His name..."**

Do you see that? God's word is a law unto Himself. He cannot oppose it. His name which is above all names is even lower than His word. In fact He is the Word as John 1 vs. 1 puts it;

**"In the beginning was the Word..." John 1:1**

The Word was here in the beginning and the Word

was God says John. So when God says His name is lower than His word don't get it wrong, all he is saying is "I am the Word". He is literally saying there is no difference between him and the word. Taking that into consideration, we see that the more word you have the more Jesus you have and the more power you possess. That is to say the more Jesus or Word you have, the more kratos you move into. This is the secret of kratos. Simple, but requires a lot of commitment.

I can assure you that if you take a good amount of hours to read the word and not foolish worldly novels and watching television you will be moving closer to kratos. You see, the word *television* itself means 'telling a vision,' but whose vision is the question? Whose vision are you following? Whose word are you feeding your spirit with?

Be grounded in the word and take hours every day to soak into it. I mean literally hours. Here I did not say books that people wrote; I am talking about the pure word as it exists in the Bible. It is in its nature inerrant and sufficient, it will cause you to propel beyond the natural abilities. One of our present day great teachers in the Lord, a man loaded with revelation, Pastor Tan, did it and the revelation that he possess boggles the mind and turns something in one's spirit. In fact when the Lord told me of these dimensions, I found out that he was one of the few that the Lord also gave the revelation to in his own way. It will move you by its own power to get the results that will not only surprise you, but those around you. This is the power of the word.

Pastor Tan spend around ten hours per day reading the Bible and praying for a full year and that changed his life. He was not reading anything else but the word. The word is powerful. In fact it is the Lord!

The Lord Jesus was the Word made flesh.

**"...the Word became flesh and dwelt among us..."
John 1:14**

Word became flesh. The Word became Jesus on earth and everything that the Word spoke would happen because the Word was the engine behind creation.

## The Speaking Word

I remember when I was in St. Lucia in the capital city, Castries, and this lady came to me with a short leg and other problems. In front of thousands of people, recorded live on camera, the Lord spoke to me and told me to speak to the leg to grow. I spoke to it and told it to grow, and there in front of all these witnesses, it grew to match the other one. The word had gained an ascending level in my spirit to such an extent that what I was now speaking was life. I was now speaking the Lord and the Lord is a Spirit and He is Life.

The Lord said;

**"The words I speak to you are spirit and they are life..." John 6:63**

He did not only say they are spirit. He said my words are life. He said don't think they are just syllabi. Know that whatever I utter is life, life in its highest form. This word life is the word 'zoe'.

Zoe means "the life as God has it". It is the life of God. The one that is actually in papa God Himself. This is the life that makes God, God. This is the life that gives Him the 'Godness' as it were.

Now He tells us that the words I speak, which are the same as the word we speak from the Bible, he says they are zoe. What? Did I hear that correctly? He says if you

41

load yourself in the word to the extent where people can not differentiate you from the word you will start babbling out life. Real life, the God life. The engine of life will kick in, He implies.

Every place where God is breathed will change. There is a pure transformation to anything that is touched by this life; a pure movement of natural cells as they are replaced by spiritual and supernatural cells. It is a life giving substance, this word we read and meditate upon.

Joshua was told...

**"...meditate upon this word and thou shalt have good success" Joshua 1:8**

### 'Good Success'

'Good success' means extra-ordinary success. It means literally to have extreme positive success that has no trace of a problem. It majors on success that adds no sorrow or success that is beyond explanation. It is the success of God.

Beloved, we should allow the word to ascend in our spirits. We should make ourselves word people and soak hour by hour in the word.

At one moment I used to tithe my time daily to prayer and then use the same hours for the word, but I have moved to where I do hours in the word and hours in prayer. I don't do it with a religious spirit, but because the word has transformed my relationship with my sweet Jesus. Boy, how I love Him so much more than I did when I first began. The word brought a great understanding, and made me intimate with my creator so that kratos is now possible and epikaizo very accessible, that I now move in it in a measure. The word is the trick.

## The Devil And Kratos

### "Jesus destroyed him who had the kratos (power)" Hebrews 2:14

Since kratos is the power of the word, the devil has his own counterfeit kratos. This is the word of deception that deceives (misleads) the spirit.

See what Apostle Paul says;

### "...deceiving the hearts of the simple..." Romans 16 vs. 18

It is possible that the words you receive can deceive your spirit. Someone might come to you and convince you that you don't even have to care about these words, yet, if you look at the book of Ephesians and read it in the Greek, you will understand that the Apostle Paul uses different words in the Greek and he plays around with these words a lot. One has to see what he meant for this power to flow. Lack of knowledge can destroy you. It can deceive the hearts of the simple. It can destroy you. The Lord God Himself says;

### "... my people perish for the lack of knowledge..." Hosea 4 vs. 6

You ought to understand revelation from the Spirit, otherwise you are dead. This might be difficult to take for;

### "the natural man cannot understand the things of the SpiritNeither can he know them FOR they are spiritually discerned" 1 Corinthians 2 vs. 14

The devil can deceive (mislead, swindle, con) by the word of deception. He will use words to persecute, to gossip, to slander, to cuss, to shout and accuse the brethren. The word says the devil IS;

**"... The accuser of the brethren..."**
**Revelation 12 vs.10**

He accuses the brethren and whosoever accuses a Christian, a man or woman of God, a brother in the church or anyone the Lord died for is an accuser of the brethren and has kratos of the devil!

That is why gossipers and accusers are dangerous people. Most times when you see them approach you, you start to fear that they will start their gossip. These people are heavily clad in this evil power that it is hard to stay around them. They carry a heavy spirit. They carry a load of accusations. They are loaded with words from the devil that they overflow with kratos, not the kratos of God, but of the devil.

Kratos of God is similar in relationship to exousia, which is also power of the word. They are much related. The devil does not possess exousia (authority), but he has kratos.

If you research wisely, you will see that the power that the devil has is borrowed from you. He can only get to use power as you give to him access. So, in a strict sense, the devil does not even possess dunamis, though some can give to you the verse that says;

**"Behold I give unto you power, over all the**
**power (dunamis) of the enemy..."**
**Luke 10 vs. 19**

They say this scripture shows the devil has power. That would be a weak point since it has to be dunamis that he gets from us human beings.

When the aforementioned verse says,

**"...the dunamis of the devil"**

...It is referring to the borrowed power like the one he got from Adam in the garden. That gave the devil a lease, which runs out when a person receives Jesus. Notice, the lease does not move his influence out of the earth; it just renders him powerless in your life. All the devil has is power, which has nothing to do with exousia (authority), ischus or dunamis. This power lies in his ability to deceive. This is his power's engine. It is his kratos, so the more I shield myself from gossip, accusation of those the Lord died for, lies and any other word from the devil, I win. I don't even need to be in the company of gossipers:

**"Blessed is the man that walketh not in the counsel of the ungodly, nor standeth in the way of sinners, or sitteth in the seat of the *scornful*"**
**Psalm 1:1**

Scornful people are gossiping people. They are jealous people and are always angry. They use the kratos of the devil; that is why the Lord blesses those who do not listen to such people. He says to those who will run away from such people:

**"...they shall be like a tree planted by the rivers; whatsoever they do shall prosper..."**
**Psalm 1:3**

The solution to this problem of the kratos of the devil is simple. You defeat him by the word. The amount of word in you determines the amount of power in you. The growth in the word determines the voltage of the kratos of God in you. It is very simple.

## Growing This Power

Meditate on the word and see how power will spill out of you. Meditate and don't stop talking the word. Speak it every day. Quote it to yourself. Read it out loud to yourself. Go in front of a mirror and talk to yourself using the word. Do it in the spirit and not religiously.

Since the devil has his own kratos, the believers should run away from gossip, slander, persecution of the brethren and all the evil words. They should run away from anyone who accuses those Christ died for. This is very important. Reading the word and understanding it by the spirit is very paramount and understanding that the devil uses words to destroy believers. So any word that does not build someone is in a way a kratos word from the devil so you avoid it.

Allow your whole being to soak into the word. Read the word of God daily, not like you do a novel but with a heart to be intimate with God and knowledge that the Lord is the word. Soak into it and believe what you read or hear in the real word of God and see how the devil will run with his tail between his knees.

CHAPTER THREE

## The Ischus Dimension For The Believer

**"And what is the immeasurable greatness of his** power (*dunamis*) **in us who believe. According to the** *ischus kratos***"**
**Ephesians 1 vs. 19**

*Ischus* is the power of **efficiency**. It is the power that gives all the dimensions efficiency. It makes the execution of power consistent.

I am sure you have experienced times when you pray or command things to happen and bam, they happen but sometimes they don't even if you cry out "in the name of Jesus" or even spell it. Things sometimes listen to your commands in the name of Jesus and sometimes they don't, yet the word says;

**"At the name of Jesus every knee should bow"**
**Philippians 2 vs. 10**

You see, the word shown there is 'meloo.' It means there is no possibility of failure, yet, you and I can testify that sometimes using the name of Jesus has not been successful when we wanted it to work causing some to doubt this verse or the whole Bible.

The problem is not in the name. It is in the *ischus*! ( power & efficiency)

Your *ischus* might not be there. You might be lacking efficiency in the power of the name. The lack of efficiency causes us to fail many times and we oppose God after

> *[handwritten: Finally, be strong in the Lord & in his mighty power .]*

we fail.

In Ephesians 6 vs. 10, the Apostle Paul says;

**"Finally be** *dunamo* *[handwritten: strong]* **in the Lord and in the strength of His** *Ischus"* *[handwritten: might]*

Apostle Paul plays around with words here as in the whole book of Ephesians. He says *"be dunamo with the kratos of the ischus"*. What could that mean? What on earth does he mean? How can one be ***dunamo*** in the **kratos** of his **ischus**?

Ischus here refers to the power associated with the power of the Holy Spirit; but now you ought to understand all power is from the Holy Spirit, but there is that resident power of the Spirit of God.

In 1 Peter chapter 4 vs. 11 it says;

**"Whosoever speaks let him speak as of the oracles of God. If one ministers, let him do it as the ability which God supplies"**

The word ability in 1 Peter 4 vs. 11 carries the same meaning as the word ischus. So it implies God or the Holy Spirit as the supplier of that power. Ischus is the working of the Holy Spirit in a believer's life. It is the efficiency brought into one's life by the Holy Spirit.

Remember the anointing is the oil of God. The anointing is from the Holy Spirit and ischus is like oil, it lubricates the flowing apparatus of God's power. It makes it flow nicely that nothing can stop it. That is why the combination of ischus and kratos produces energy;

*[handwritten: incomparably great power]*
**"...greatness of his** *dunamis* **in us who believe according to the** *eneges* **of his** *ischus kratos"*
**Ephesians 1 vs. 19-20** *[handwritten: mighty strength]*
*[handwritten: working]*

This tells us that kratos (invincibility) and ischus (efficiency) brings energy, which the Greek New Testament calls *energeo*. It is this efficiency (ischus) that makes kratos flow and the increase of these two as they relate causes explosive power. It causes *energeo*. It brings energy to the system and the name of Jesus then has no blockage. It will flow and work every time when ischus is developed.

Let's look at God Himself using ischus;

**"They shall suffer the punishment of eternal destruction and exclusion from the presence of the Lord and from the glory of his might (ischus) 2 Thess. 1 vs. 9**

The Lord here through the Apostle is saying the ischus gives order to the system and anyone that will choose to be rebellious will suffer the absence of this glue that makes the whole system efficient. He is saying hell is the absence of ischus. It is the presence of chaos. So, where ischus is, there is order, there is efficiency, there is ischus, and there is the power of efficiency.

## Increasing Ischus

Ischus is the power that relies on prayer and character. It is the inward working power of the Holy Spirit into your life. It is the Holy Spirit working in you. So its main power comes from the character built through prayer. Remember the sons of Sceva;

**And there were seven sons of one Sceva, a Jew, and chief of the priests, which did so. And the evil spirit answered and said, Jesus I know, and Paul I know; but who are ye? And the man in whom the evil spirit was leaped on them, and overcame them, and prevailed against them, so that they**

**fled out of that house naked and wounded (Acts 19 vs. 14-16).**

The demons beat them up and exposed them and made them march naked for all to see and laugh at. The trick here is found in the name they called out. That name of Jesus! They thought the power was in the sound of the name. They were confused. They had missed the point. Power in the name of Jesus is not just in how you call it. If it were so, the demons would have left, but that was not the case. The book of Acts tells us plainly that they were beaten up heavily and the demons gained ascend over them.

The word 'NAME' in the following verse;

**"...At the** *NAME* **of Jesus every knee should bow..."**
**Philippians 2 vs.10**       Anoma

The name refers to the word '*anoma,*' which means *character, nature,* and *characteristic* of Jesus. So the demons could only be cast out when the character of Jesus was built first by the word and intensified by prayer *ischus*; and without this, the sons of Sceva could be many among us!

Without the character of Jesus, the ***anoma***, the nature of Jesus, demons do not have the rule or commandment to obey you. The sons of Sceva thought the sound of the name of Jesus was the key, yet this was a deception. It wasn't even close. Their characters stank and the demons could smell it from miles away and they refused to follow.

**"...Jesus I know, Paul I know, who are you?"**
**Acts 19 vs. 15**

Do you see that? They said 'they **know**'. They were

very much aware of Jesus and similarly aware of Paul's character, which was just like Jesus, but did not understand the nature of the sons of Sceva. The demons attacked them and saw their chance to attack them as great based upon their characters.

Their characters might have been good in human analysis, but the demons were looking for the character of Jesus and when they found none, they jumped on the seven sons and beat them up. They were attacked and made a spectacle of. Their character reported them.

### Prayer: The Builder

Prayer builds character. When you are a man of character, your character can be seen even in your words. You become efficient in your dealings with people. You become humble because prayer would have taught you to be at ease in the Lord.

### Ischus In My life Experiences

Here I am going to give just one example of character built in prayer. This character swallows up pride.

When I went to Africa, Zimbabwe I met a man who was so submitted to the Holy Spirit that one could sense it from afar. He had this **anoma** that one day another Pastor in the same city who did not like him because of jealousy, mentioned this humble pastors name in church, and demons had a field day with him. They began to literally shout and beat him up. This Pastor tried to cast them out in the name of Jesus but nothing happened. The demons were still at it, like the sons of Sceva they did not recognise this Pastor's authority. At first the whole thing was confusing but it changed when they began to speak. And here is what they said of this man, "we are running away from Prophet E.

Makandiwa, and you start mentioning his name" The name of Prophet E Makandiwa just by being mentioned was giving them torment so they came out of the people and thought they could find rest in this other Pastor's church only to hear the Pastor mention the Prophet's name. The demons recognised two things; Prophet E. Makandiwa had the **anoma** of Jesus so they ran away from his church but also understood that they would find peace in the churches that opposed Prophet Makandiwa. Oh, what a testimony to have!

This Prophet who happens to be a best friend and a brother of mine, since we share the same spiritual father, has been used to do extra ordinary miracles including raising up the dead all because of Ischus and Kratos which feeds power to the dunamis the Lord gave him. Many times he has been moved by grace into the Epikaizo dimension which we will discuss later in detail. He is not the one who does these things; it is God Himself who chooses when to use him.

Remember Apostle Paul says "be dunamo with the kratos of the ischus". What could that mean? What on earth does he mean? How can one be **dunamo** in the **kratos** of his **ischus**? This happens when a believer gets the word to soak into them and prayer life increased to the extent where this power and character of the believer starts to grow the level of his dunamis. That being said means Prophet Makandiwa's dunamis was loaded with kratos of the ischus. He was now *dunamo* with *kratos* of the *ischus* as Apostle Paul puts it!

Now, ischus builds one's character. It humbles one and gets them to rely on the Lord only. Prayerful people are people of few words for they use most of their words in prayer. They are people of character. They are not ashamed to say what the Lord has done for them for they are people of prayer. When the Lord used me to impart on him, this man did not hold his peace. When the Lord used him to impart on me, I did not hold my peace. Not because of the people but because of the character built in me by prayer, ischus. When I met this Prophet, my church was growing but not the way I knew it should and he sat me down in the word and read the word to me, shared what the Lord told him. He got down to the word and living a holy life and all the other principles for growth. This changed my church. It was all based on the word. He was imparting to me the kratos through getting deep into the word with regards to growing my church both in number and in spiritual growth. He was used by God to impart into my life that which made him a man of mega churches and power and my church changed completely that within a space of a few months we were adding chairs upon chairs, even moving from our building to one that was three times bigger.

When I met him, his prophetic was not at my level and I imparted to Him what the Lord has given me in abundance and that is the Prophetic and his prophetic was unlocked into greater heights that he is now a man with precision when it comes to the prophetic. This I did through the word and through prayer just as he had done with regards to what I lacked. NOW, WHILST I am at it let me say something very important. The church here is missing it. Many are lazy to commit to the word and deep prayer so they have created doctrines that confuse many.

Impartation is not giving someone something God did not give them but a sharing of the prayer life and other areas that have worked for one. No one can give you a gift. That is not possible. What we can do is inform each other on how we have sharpened things in our walk with the Lord and from those lessons we commit to a prayer life that matches or goes even further than the one who is telling us their prayer life that would have caused them to excel in the gifting or blessing. No one can give you what God did not give you. Believers should not

53

be lazy. We should be dedicated to prayer. When I met the man of God he was already prophesying. In fact he started prophesying at a young age but God had blessed me with a lot of grace concerning the prophetic that I had a lot of spiritual principles that could help heighten someone's prayer life in line with the prophetic and he had principles that could aid my prayer life with regards to what he helped me with. It's all experience obtained through prayer and word, nothing less. There is no other secret to power than the dimensions that God set in motion.

I started realising and prophesying in grade 2, at the age of seven, so I had walked with God in this line more than other people and had amassed a lot of principles and developed a sunesis and phronesis concerning the prophetic. With experience and the word we sharpened each other and in prayer we asked God to sharpen us. Christians are now too lazy; they want things to just come.

See, I was born a prophet and that is the foundation but sharpening my gift requires a little effort from me. I call it little because all things are under God's sovereign will. No one can give you a gift. No person, no matter how anointed, can make you a prophet or an evangelist. Only God can do that, with your prayer as the glue that cements everything. My sharpness in the prophetic and in healing was due to God and myself getting closer through prayer and a lifestyle that came out of a walk with Him and it is this lifestyle that I give to one who is already a prophet so they can sharpen their gift to my level. It is a matter of principles built through prayer and an experience obtained for years that makes one able to unlock someone's office to higher levels.

The idea that a gift or a calling can be given by just laying on of hands is simply ignorance gone rampage! To say such will be the longest way of saying nonsense.

The word creates humility; one begins to know they need others when they have the word. Whether it is the prophetic or growth in ministry or power to do miracles, signs and wonders, these things come when one is fully stationed in the word. When one is in the word, they possess a keen understanding of spiritual things. They begin to understand that;

**"Iron sharpens iron..." Proverbs 27 vs. 17**

Now for iron to sharpen iron, there should be a realisation that the iron should get that it is blunt in other areas otherwise it will think it needs no sharpening at all. Iron can only be sharpened when it says it is not sharp in other areas. I was not sharp in other areas and other powerful men of faith I respect have sharpened me. He was not as sharp as I was in other areas and through the word and prayer God came to our rescue. It's just that people already think they know so they do not give themselves to the word and to prayer.

My spiritual father Prophet Victor Kusi Boateng, is a word and prayer man. He can pray for days upon days and be in word for days, just studying and listening to God. He could not speak in English because he did not go to school like we did but after fasting for almost a year, dedicating his time to prayer and the word of God, he woke up one day and he could speak English. The Lord touched his tongue through prayer. Prayer changes things.

I love prayer and I love the word of God so much that I talk it. I sleep it. I drink it. I think the word and nothing less and that is why I am being used in a higher dimension in the prophetic and other signs and wonders. Any powerful man of God will be a witness to this. It's all because of the word and prayer. Nothing outside the word can work. My spiritual father taught me to make the word of God the standard for my life no matter the persecution I face. I have learnt from the word and to be a stickler with regards to prayer. I have been taught well and got the right foundation of prayer. Through prayer we have been taught to love by the Holy Ghost that we do not breakdown in the face of persecution. Prayer made everything that people see possible.

Humility built through the word and prayer makes it possible to receive a man with fewer church members than the ones you have and admit that I need what you have. That is what he did and the Lord said because of his humility it was possible to get what he got.

A time of prayer is where one releases their entire burden and leaves with nothing to bare so there is no pressure or anger. People that have too many things in their hearts are always troubled. That is why there are some diseases called 'rush' diseases. These are illnesses worsened by anxiety, but where prayer is, there is no anxiety.

See the word says;

**"...he that keeps you will neither sleep nor slumber"**
**Psalm 121 vs. 3**

So prayer teaches you that God listens every minute and he doesn't sleep nor slumber. So you begin to realise that if God does not sleep there is no need to not find sleep. He himself does not sleep. He does not even doze off so there is no reason for the two of us to be awake all the time. I will pray and rest and He does the rest. In prayer, I let go and let God. In prayer you have to let go and let God deal with it. So depression will never come knocking.

If this character gets built up, demons will recognize your invincibility, your kratos by specifics. You become clean through prayer.

I tell you, do 10 hours or so per day for a year and see how you will turn into a 'bullet' of a believer. Your efficiency will be increased so much that the devil will not understand what hit him. Your ischus will be great.

Many believers are spiritual Vacso Da Gama's. They are simply the Columbus kind. They start by just checking out churches and ministers and that's not ischus. They attend numerous different churches in the space of a year and are never satisfied. Ischus is the power that lubricates spiritual laws and causes kratos to block natural laws.

Ischus has a lot to do with character. With ischus you have temperance;

**"...add temperance..."**
**2 Peter 1 vs. 6**

*Temperance* here is "ENKRAITEA," which means to hold oneself from within. It refers to the hand of your spirit grabbing you so you can be a peaceable person, as well as hold and sustain a good character. ENKRAETIA – hold yourself from within. It is the kratos power from within that aids it by moving the hand of the Spirit to hold you from inside and control you. It controls your temper and puts a smile on your face. It does wonders to your character and all this happens when time is spent in prayer before the Lord.

I remember when I started in the Lord. I did not like prayer. I liked the fact that I was born again but the idea of spending hours in prayer was just nonsense to me. I could not conceive why it would be necessary.

This is when I met some folk who thought everything is predestined. They thought all we are is just some robots and God was the remote controller busy controlling us robots. I just couldn't understand, then, why I needed to pray. I figured if God has written it before hand, then there is no need for me to be a person of prayer, but that was far from the truth. God wants intimacy. I began to read the word on my own and realised that God was consistent. He said;

**"...Whosoever will, let him come..."**
**Revelation 22 vs. 17**

That single verse led me into a search. He wanted me to come to Him if I will. Not just if He wills, but if I want. I, Uebert Angel, had a duty now to fulfil. I needed to be there if I wanted. That understanding and revelation made me look for an intimate way to relate to Him. I saw that I needed Him to permeate my body and I asked, and boy did He give me more than I thought possible. I was willing and I came to Him and He gave.

I immediately became a man of prayer and my temper, which had previously been poisonous, abated. I could be set off by any little thing, but prayer got me to a level of peace where silence is the order.

With prayer and the word, you become a man of few words and a lot of character and with character, power flows freely, for ischus is a lubricator. It is the power of efficiency developed by prayer. It relies on character too.

### Consistency

Ischus is the power of efficiency. This means it relies on consistency for things to be efficient. If one wants effectiveness, they will have automatically asked for efficiency.

Consistency in attending church, consistency in giving tithes and offering as well as alms, consistency in love, in peace and in character. All in all, be consistent in every aspect of your life. Let your life expose consistency. There are people you and I know who have serious mood swings. One day, they are very cheerful and the next they are bitter. If persecution comes, they will break down and seek ways of revenging. Not with me, I do not care what my enemies say. I have been to the school of the Holy Ghost and he taught me through prayer to have a character of Christ. I am not perturbed. I do not fear people. I am consistent in my response to persecution because prayer taught me to be humble and to be peaceful.

Be consistent, be a self starter. Don't leave everything for others to do. God is looking for HOT PEOPLE!

Who among us with a two plate stove that has one hot plate and one cold, will use the cold one to cook a meal? That person would be stupid. God is not a man that He can be a fool. He will also use hot people.

God uses consistent people; so if you want a life of miracles, a life of ischus – be consistent. Not one day you are in church, the other you are out of it. The next day you are in another church and the following week you have quit. Be mature. Be consistent. Consistency is efficiency and efficiency is ischus.

# CHAPTER FOUR

## Dunamis

The power that explodes bullets - Dunamis. It is a supernatural power plant **only** legal and available to believers. It is the inherent power that every dimension feeds into. The higher it is the more extraordinary things a man can perform through the Spirit of God. Many live within its potential yet beneath its power. With this power nothing will be impossible. Anything becomes possible: the sick will be healed, you will see the unseen, say the unsaid, tell the untold, mountains will move and demons will flee. The generic definition of dunamis is: the dynamic power to cause changes. It is an explosive power!

## Tormenting Ability

Dunamis is God's supernatural ability inside the believer. You see, *dunamis* is where we get dynamite. It is an explosive power; it is a spiritual chemical explosive.

An explosive is anything that once ignited burns extremely fast and produces a large amount of hot gas in the process. The hot gas then expands and applies pressure.

Now, the Lord has given us dunamis which is better than this. This chemical explosion of the heavens expands and applies pressure until an explosion happens. That was why the demons begged the Lord Jesus to let them go;

**"...are you come to torment us..."**
**Matthew 8 vs. 29**

They knew if one has dunamis, he would have tormenting ability. They became aware that this Jesus had tormenting ability and if he was to use it a spiritual chemical explosion would happen. Even to this day, demons are very aware of this very fact. They cannot mess the real believer up. They are afraid of a believer who knows they possess this power. This is the explosive and tormenting ability.

This dynamite or dunamis power from heaven cannot work on its own. It has to have all the other dimensions working at least in a measure for things to take place. You see, you need exousia, kratos, and ischus for it to at least begin to work. A lot of people would say dynamite can just blow up then so should this power. That would be a lie.

You see, dynamite is simply some sort of absorbent material like sawdust soaked in nitro-glycerine. The absorbent material makes the nitro-glycerine much more stable. A blasting cap is then used in many cases to detonate dynamite. Blasting the cap then causes a small explosion that triggers the larger explosion in the dynamite itself. It is a web of connections that ought to work first before anything happens, just like the dunamis from on high. It needs other principle dimensions of power to function. If you don't apply other dimensions you will not have an explosion, but an implosion.

### Implosion Of Dunamis

Dunamis if not used in connection with other dimensions will fail to blow up when commanded to. This causes many believers to live a mediocre life. They don't know why things don't work. They are always looking to blame others. If a believer does not put explosive power onto a person they pray for, they implode and oppose the person for lack of faith. That, many times is an implosion of dunamis. Sometimes, yes indeed the persons faith is to blame. That too is an implosion of dunamis on the part of the sick person.

Dunamis relies on authority (*exousia*), *ischus* (power of efficiency), and *kratos* (power of invincibility) for it to do its work.

Dynamite itself is different and made up of different forms that make it stable or unstable. This is the same for dunamis; it can be dangerous if unstable. Use it well otherwise, you might blame the Lord and be offended when things don't form up the way you want them to, all because you did not adhere to the Lord's commandments.

Dynamite also needs a detonator which in the spiritual world is the faith obtained through the word and the switch on the detonator is *exousia*. Authority will release the power.

**Dunamis** then is the ability imparted by God on the believer; and if it is imparted ability, it shows that it is a part of God's ability. A part of God's dynamite. This is the actual power, strength, might, and true ability coming from God. It's undiluted! Boy I love Jesus!

## Increasing Dunamis

All the dimensions when they grow are in all the senses feeding power into dunamis so to grow dunamis is to get yourself stationed in the other dimensions and that causes dunamis to grow. Speaking in tongues and singing in tongues increases dunamis. Dunamis has a connection and strong relationship with authority or *exousia*. However, *dunamis* is empowered by the Holy Spirit; that is why scripture says;

**"Ye shall receive DUNAMIS when the Holy Ghost Is come upon you"**
**Acts 1 vs. 8**

The Holy Spirit is the engine behind all the dimensions by being specifically related to this one called dunamis. That shows us the increasing of it has to be directly related to the source, the Holy Spirit. The best way then becomes speaking and singing in tongues, all in the spirit and getting stationed into all dimensions. Notice that dunamis is inherent power. It is the source of the power of a believer that can be increased when other dimensions are increased. Many other things associated with dimensions can create a song by the spirit, singing it by the Spirit, and making a spiritual melody and a rhythmic dance authored by the Spirit. Anything short of this will not do much.

## Edification: Tongues, recharging in progress

In the Greek, the word edification means recharging as if a person performing the act was a battery. This is a recharging of spiritual cells, if you like.

Paul said:

**"I thank God that I speak in tongues more than all of you..."**
**1 Corinthians 14 vs.18**

If it was good for Paul why can it not be right for us? If he thanked God openly about having this gift, this recharging ability, why can we not speak these same tongues? God Himself says, "Do not forbid the speaking of tongues" for they are a generating power for the Dunamis. Tongues enact the dimensional growth of the

Exousia that gives authority to use the Dunamis.

God had two things in mind when He gave that command. He knew we would say that tongues are not for this day and age and He ultimately knew their purpose, edifying or building oneself. God does not end there, He adds in His word:

**"He who speaks in tongues, speaks to God for no one understands him"**
**1 Corinthians 14 vs. 2**

This way of prayer is the only prayer the devil cannot understand; he cannot understand anything that is said, and neither can he perceive what you are asking God to do for you, nor can he lip read the mysteries.

Daniel was told by the angel that for twenty one days the devil prevented him from coming with the answer to his prayer. Why? It is simple, the devil understood his prayer, for he could not speak in tongues; that ability was given to us in Acts 2 vs. 3 and 4.

**"And there appeared unto them cloven tongues like as of fire, and it sat upon each of them. And they were all filled with the Holy Ghost, and began to speak with other tongues, as the Spirit gave them utterance" (Acts 2 vs. 3-4).**

And;

**"Behold I give you power"**
**Luke 10 vs. 19**

This Dunamis can be employed to execute judgement or wrath and at the same time can be used to perform signs and wonders. This supernatural power that explodes bullets is the one our Lord Jesus Christ gave you and I. It is ours by right, though acquired through grace, note:

I said by right. It is the same power He possesses and since it is no longer us that live but Christ who lives in us, then we, apart from being God carriers, have become possessors of the dunamis of God.

See, this brothers and sisters is not a suggestion but a divine fact. Dunamis is the power that bulldozes mountains, opens the deaf ear, opens the eye of the blind, parts Red seas and raises the dead. Though you might not know it, you already possess this power, if you are a Holy Spirit filled Christian (Mark 16 vs. 17); but as you continue to see, it needs the other dimensions of power to increase steadily.

Understand this; the power that explodes bullets is wrapped in us for the common good. This is no longer a mystery to be put under the theological microscope; it is a reality. You can heal the sick, restore sight, be prosperous financially, physically, make the blind see and profit withal. Brothers and sisters, we are the new creation - the new supermen, the unheard of, unique, and never seen before creatures. We are God carriers - God Himself in His entire splendour lives in the inside of us.  Now, anything is possible!

By holding this book, I do not only believe, but I know deep down you have a surge running through you, compelling you towards a profound need to live a victorious life, help the sick, and perform the miraculous. God has a commission and is ready to let you walk in your right place as the son of the Most High, full of power, signs and wonders.

All this for your own information is done through the power that already works in us. The power is not coming from anywhere; it is already in you but works outwardly to affect not only yourself but also a change in your world.

Ischus and kratos work on the inside. Exousia like dunamis works close together on the outside.

This, as you are seeing, is not power you were waiting for to come from heaven. If you were, I am sorry to say, you wasted a lot of time and you missed it; for the word maintains that God:

**"...is able to do exceedingly, abundantly more than you can ever ask or think through the power that works IN US" (Ephesians 3 vs. 20).**

Keep speaking the language of the Holy Spirit. Keep singing it with melody derived from your inner being.

## Dunamis Is Already In The Inside Of You

Remember God could have clenched another fist of soil to make Eve, He could have said a word and Eve could have come into being but He did not. Why?

**"Now the Lord God said, it is not good (sufficient, satisfactory) that the man should be alone; I will make him a (helper) help meet (suitable, adapted, and complementary) for him...And the Lord God caused a deep sleep to fall upon Adam; and while he slept; He took one of his ribs ... and closed up the [place with] flesh".**
**Genesis 2 vs. 18, 21 (AMP)**

This is evidence enough that God knew that everything we ever need is already on the inside of us, wrapped in the very being of who we are, begging to be let out into the open. God did not need to create anything from anywhere else; in fact the scriptures agree that God said after creating everything:

**"...it was good..."**

Now listen, God's *'it is good'* is not an *'it might be good'* statement. He meant it! Everything we need is already in us, it has already been completed in the spiritual realm; what is left for us is to harness the Dunamis within us; grow it through intertwining it with ischus, kratos, and exousia and translate those things that are in the spiritual realm, from that realm into the natural.

Notice when God said '...it was good...' He confirmed that everything present at that time was able to provide for the need of common good and that nothing was to be further created so as to provide for the needs of the creatures that were already there. In a very broad sense, God was proclaiming that the creative power rests with one of these creatures He had created, (Adam to be specific). The proof for it became the creation of Eve.

See! You have the Dunamis of God. Every Spirit filled Christian has it. Dunamis is the bullet of God. Exousia on the other hand, is His gun.

Now there is no need to walk with a long face and anticipate defeat anymore. God has given us power like none other. In reality we are walking gods for every creature produces after its own kind. Dogs give birth to dogs, cats to cats, lion to lions, chickens to chickens and God to gods. My Lord Jesus Christ said it best:

**"... ye are gods..."**
**John 10 vs. 34**

Dunamis shows the life of God in us. It provokes *zoe* in us, the life of God.

Apart from ZOE, meaning the life of God, it also means the life as God has it. This means if God can command things into existence, I can also command things into existence, since I have this zoe on the inside of me.

## Crusade In Africa

On my visit to Africa, thousands were in attendance and this zoe life was evident as miracle after miracle, testimony after testimony came flooding in. People's names, addresses, telephone numbers, future events that have so far come to pass and strict direction for their lives came from within me as the God kind of life showed that it was well acquainted with my spirit. The five dimensions of power were working simultaneously in my life just like they should in yours. Scores were healed of life threatening diseases all for the glory of the living God. Believers should not be sick.

Is Jesus sick? No. So we should not be sick. Is He broke? No. So we should not be poor. We are like our Lord Jesus for the word says "As He is, so are we" (1 John 4:17). Look! Even when there came before Him time to pay taxes, God placed a coin in the mouth of a fish. The Lord never held a funeral service; people could not die around Him. He was never sick. The diseases were afraid of Him and they are afraid of you and me too.

For example, when I began to pray for the sick the Lord told me to look into people's eyes and they in turn had to fasten their eyes on mine, just like Peter and John commanded the lame man at the gate called Beautiful. When they did, the demons would scream out of them and completely deaf people started hearing. The Lord showed up in a mighty way because dunamis was intertwined with other dimensions. It grew because dimensions feed power into dunamis.

## The Mystery Of Dunamis

Dunamis, when it was given to believers, signified and still signifies the possession of God. God has possessed the believer. We are now possessed by a greater power called God. Dunamis then is God possessing us!!!

Notice, with dunamis, we are no longer the ones who are living, but Christ who lives and performs miracles in us. So, there is absolutely no way we cannot have victory. There is also absolutely no way things will not work. We possess power to explode bullets.

The Holy Ghost Himself through these pages is showing you how to reach all the dimensions of supernatural power so you can have success in your faith life. See what Paul says here:

**"I am crucified with Christ: nevertheless I live; YET NOT I, but Christ lives in me: and the life which I now live in the flesh I live by the FAITH OF THE SON OF GOD (The God-kind of faith)" (Galatians 2:20).**

Now, if Paul says "I am crucified", then I know I am dead, but when he *changes* tempo and starts saying "nevertheless I live, yet not I" - I am compelled to find out who "I" or who "ME" is. However, Paul does not waste time in answering this question. He says in plain language "ME is Christ". He simply says Christ is the one who lives and I am dead so if I am dead and Christ is the one who lives, then you if you are a believer, you are... You can finish off the sentence on your own!

If you look at that verse again, you will see that you died with Christ, but you did not rise; only Christ did. See, it is Christ that lives, not you. It is high time believers understood the generic language of scripture. Here I am NOT saying we are Christ Jesus and or that He does not matter, GOD FORBID, we are not Him but He has possessed us. That is why we can have explosive power.

Way back, there was a lady by the name Mariah Woodworth-

Etter, who was so endowed with dunamis that when she came to town to preach, scores of people miles away would fall under the power of the Spirit because this lady was in town. The dimensions of power were too much on her. It was explosive. She had the power to explode demons.

Another man who was too possessed with God was John G. Lake, who when there was an outbreak of a disease he called scientists to put viruses on his hands and observe what would happen. Right there before their eyes and to their astonishment, the dunamis on him killed the disease. He was loaded with dunamis from on high.

## Miracles Can't Help Themselves But Show Up!

Dunamis is a power house for the believer!

Another lady that carried a lot of this amazing power was Kathryn Kuhlman. One day she could not use the main door to the church because of the many people that came to the crusade; so she was told to use another entrance that passed through the kitchen, and as she passed through the kitchen, the kitchen staff in their numbers fell down under the dunamis of the Lord, unbelievers and believers alike. *Dunamis* did not choose.

Dunamis is the power plant given to the believer by the Lord; but it has to relate to all other dimensions of power for it to work effectively. Dunamis is the proof that we have become GOD CARRIERS. You carry God around and miracles can't help themselves but show up. For the God in me has faith, His own kind of faith. God has dunamis and since He lives in me He has to use His dunamis to perform His will, and the amount of it in me is determined by how I relate my dunamis to other dimensions of God's power!

The Bible says

**"Greater is He that is in you, than he that is in the world."**
**1 John 4 vs. 4**

That means that my body has become a carrier of a greater power than the devil and all his cohorts fear; since God is LOVE (I John 4:8) and within Love there is trust and hope, I will win all the time with His faith. Look at what Paul says about what Love really is:

**1 Corinthians 13:7...**
**"...always TRUSTS, always HOPES, always PERSEVERES ..."**

**Love never FAILS!**

In order to have this dimension of dunamis, we MUST have a deeper revelation of God.

## Dunamis -
## The Disease Repelling Power

The day you and I were born again, God implanted a form of blood type that repels diseases, breaks the venom of every known and unknown virus and cuts to pieces the yoke of bondage. The anointing upon your life is a yoke breaking and burden removing anointing, which will bring rivers to your desert. John, under the inspiration of the Holy Spirit, cried out and said:

**"You have an anointing within you and**
**You know all things"**
**(1 John 2 vs. 20).**

We know the reality of what God has done over our lives and it is that truth we know that makes us free. But you see, I never say believers can't get sick. No, I do not say that. What I say is that 'we don't get sick'. This is very different from 'we can't get sick' in that the latter shows that it is impossible to be sick, but that would be a lie from the pits of hell. The former which is correct says 'we don't get sick' meaning that it is not in the nature of Christ for a believer to be sick because dunamis is the power that transforms your mortal body by giving it a spiritual ascent.

However, some believers may get sick; but when they get sick, there are truths in the word that can get them direct proof that will confront the disease. Here it is:

**"By His stripes we are healed..."**
**Isaiah 53 vs. 5**

When Isaiah spoke it back in the Old Testament, it was still being fulfilled and it was a truth that was prophetic. But when Peter says it, he utters it in the past tense. He says:

**"By His stripes ye were healed"**
**1 Peter 2 vs. 24**

Do you see the difference in revelation? Isaiah is including himself in the benefits but Peter says He has already benefited BECAUSE of how powerful dunamis is, so he simply says *"ye were healed...,"* when Isaiah says *"we are healed"*. Peter puts it in the past tense by using *"were,"* whereby Isaiah is using *"are."* This is a sure revelation on the supernatural power of a believer, the supernatural dunamis of the believer. We are loaded with dynamic power, DUNAMIS, to cause a change in every area of our different situations.

The problem is that many New Testament people live even lower than the Old Testament folks, and that is not flattering. It undermines the dunamis in them.

## Finally

As you begin to exercise the dunamis in you, let it work alongside the other dimensions of power. Tell yourself, 'I am not stopping here. I am growing more and more in the dimensions of the God given power in me.'

As you shall see in the next chapter, dunamis works quite closely to *exousia.*

See, some folks in the Old Testament lived better than believers in that they got a hold of the New Testament Revelation on dunamis long before it was given in the New Testament. They touched the hem of Jesus' garment by their spirit back in the Old Testament so that they started living like us here in the New Testament, who have dunamis on a daily basis.

Look at Moses; He still had his power at the age of 120 even though he did not have the Holy Spirit in him.

Moses testified;
**...His eye was not dim neither was his strength abated.**
**Deuteronomy 34 vs. 7**

That was Dunamis Power that gave him enablement!

CHAPTER FIVE

## The Believer's Authority: Exousia

They eat raw meat. The muscles of these people flex with every heart beat. They enhance their strength with drugs, 'hibited' or prohibited. They pump iron till they ache. They lift weights. In all senses, they carry another type of dunamis (power). We all know them...they are rugby players, yet in the middle of the pitch stands a skinny figure with no muscles, a whistle between his lips - we know him too, he is the referee.

The players have all the dunamis to lift him up; yet the EXOUSIA to give the red card belongs to this lean figurine, the referee. The players with all their power are not omnipotent on the pitch, but the referee is. He has both the dunamis and the exousia. He can give a yellow card or a red card and at the same time have authority to boot out any player according to his own discretion. Authority, though it looks like power, is not dunamis, but simply the legal right to exercise dunamis.

This Exousia is still where it has always been and that is in Jesus Christ; and Jesus Christ is also still where He said He will be, and that is, in us. We are Jesus carriers. We have become God carriers. In fact, He lives in us and through us, and so the exousia to use dunamis to perform miracles lives within us. Glory be to God!

You see, a robber can possess as many guns as he wants, but without the bullets to go with the guns, the guns are useless. He can clothe himself in police attire and stand his ground; but only a policeman who has the badge and the record will show he has the authority to apprehend the counterfeit.

A counterfeit note can have all the colours of a real bill and might have been printed by the same machine as the real one but only the bill with a reserve identification number, water mark, and a strip, can buy. Any person can have a gun, but the one with a loaded one has the real power.

### Caution On Exousia And Dunamis

It is necessary to warn you about the problem of coveting the spectacular, rather than the supernatural. It is very dangerous to have spasms of emotion aimed at unlocking and possessing the power to perform miracles without taking into your spirit the message of the Cross.

Miracles are meant to point people to Christ and not for show, which is exactly why John called them signs; because he got a revelation on the purpose of a miracle… to point people to the Lord. It is for this same purpose that God has called me and others to tell His body how to harness the dunamis power in you, placed there by God, the author and finisher of our faith, Jesus Christ and how to use exousia to implement it.

### Exousia

Exousia means authority to control. It reflects ability giving jurisdiction. This is the power to rule over something. It is the power that grants judicial precedence.

The New Testament Greek Lexicon defines exousia as the power of choice, liberty of doing as one pleases. It all gives a meaning that denotes ability to influence and of right or privilege.

In short, this is the power of rule or government. This is the power of those whose will and command must be submitted to by others and obeyed. That is talking about you and me controlling those things obeyed, because we have been blessed with exousia.

Exousia is in many facets and covers many areas;

*It is universally* authority against being controlled by mankind. *It is specifically* power to manage domestic affairs or judicial decisions, or any specific thing that the boundary of authority covers. **This is the higher level** – superior to mere human beings, giving spiritual potentates.

Exousia extends to mean the legal authority or a crown. One who has exousia is King. This is what was communicated powerfully in the book of Revelation;

## "...He has made us Kings..." Revelation 1:6

Christ made us kings and queens so we could exercise authority over our circumstances and over demons and the devil. His making us kings, queens, and priests shows that there is an authority now behind us. It concurs that we have exousia, since kings possess a level of authority here on earth. The Bible says, who can oppose what a king or queen has decreed?

The words of a king have authority. The words of a queen carry authority that requires the subjects to submit. We have that power. We possess that authority and the devil and his gang understand it. They know it so they cannot play games with us.

Any believer who understands the power in them is a dangerous Christian to the enemy.

Some say, "I don't care about this exercise of exousia, all I know is I am saved and I believe in Jesus, that's all

I need". That will be crazy. For one, you are wrong that believing in God is enough. It is not!

See this scripture of the bible;

**"...believe in God thou hast done well, but the devil also believes..."**
**James 2 vs. 19**

The believing stage is ok, but not at all too different to what demons do. There is a further stage of going beyond and exercising that power, exercising that authority, exercising that exousia.

When you exercise exousia your believing now is solid. It should not just end on believing though. The devils do the same and they tremble, but that does not chase them away. What chases them away is the right, authority, privilege, power of control in you to cast them out; and they will respond, otherwise you will be filled with the sons of Sceva disease. They did not have authority to use the name of Jesus, not even that of Paul, but tried to cast out a demon. You know what the demons uttered;

**"Jesus I know, Paul I know who are you..." Acts 19:15**

The demons knew the authority of Jesus and knew the authority that Paul carried in Christ; so they were searching for the same thing in the sons of Sceva, but boy, they did not find any exousia. They beat the sons of Sceva because the Jesus authority was not found in them. There was no power behind their authority.

## Power Behind Authority

One most important thing believers forget is that there should be some form of power in the one giving you exousia; otherwise the exousia would be nothing. Power which is very absolute should be behind the control or governance for it to be listened to.

The Lord Jesus said

**"...All authority (exousia) has been given unto me in heaven and earth" (Matthew 28 vs. 18).**

The Lord said he had absolute authority from papa God Himself and that carried the power of exousia. It had a powerful source. The C.E.O of the universe was the source of exousia, not some angel somewhere, but God was behind all the exousia on the Lord Jesus Christ. This is something to understand clearly.

Here the Lord Jesus becomes a channel through which the Father's every purpose and plan is worked out. Christ possesses authority backed up by a mighty source who is God. I say this knowing full well that Christ and the father are one, but remembering also that Christ said;

**"He emptied himself and took on the form of a servant..."**
**Philippians 2 vs. 7**

So, what He emptied supplied the power behind his authority when He was here on earth. It is most blessed to know this truth that our authority then is backed up by the resurrected Christ. So, our words are not in vain. Our exousia is not something to play around with, but an explosive jurisdiction which all creation has to listen to, since we carry something of their creator. Do you see how marvellous this truth is?

## The Power And The Authority

The other dimensions of power like ischus, kratos, and dunamis which the Lord gives, have to be in you in a measure or without measure (if that is possible), for your authority to be absolute. One cannot just have authority and do the job. Your authority works when you have something to enforce it with. The enemy has to fear something happening to them if they don't obey.

If you look at a policeman, he can stop you and you will stop; not because you just like stopping, but you know if you don't, you'll have massive problems. So you see, your obedience is following a clear understanding that if I don't stop, I am going to jail or will be fined. Here what you fear more is the consequence based upon the power of the source of his authority, which in this case would be the federal government or her majesty the Queen, or another government somewhere. All you fear in your deepest sense is the source; but since the source has delegated its authority to the policeman, you in turn fear the policeman so you obey!

As a believer, the source is Jesus the resurrected Christ, the one who rose from the dead, defeated the devil, conquered death, raised from the dead, seated at the throne of grace, etc.; this is my source and the devil knows it, so he trembles at the sight of me. What he is afraid of is my exousia; based on the source of that exousia, which is Jesus, who has already beaten him for all time.

The devil knows this fact, so now he is afraid of you since your source and you have become one. You have the authority of the source so there is no longer any difference. You are now explosive. It is now as though Jesus were here on earth calling the shots Himself.

In fact the word says He is here;

**"...behold I am with you always..."**
**Matthew 28 vs. 20**

So, when a believer enacts exousia, the devil sees Jesus in the believer and runs. The believer's authority has just taken precedence based upon the source of the exousia.

See, if the source is weak, the exousia is weak; but if the source is strong, the exousia is also very strong.

## The Relationship BETWEEN Jesus, Exousia, And Dunamis

In the United States of America, there was this company that had an advertising campaign, which made a lot of impact. The advert read;

"When X Company speaks everybody listens".

This advert would feature scores of people walking in the streets going about their day to day business and as soon as the name of the company was mentioned like 'X!' immediately everybody in the street, regardless of what they were doing, would stop still in their tracks and listen. No matter how busy these people were, the commercial would indicate that they would stop when the name was called out.

This was a very successful campaign. It was a success advert. This is similar to what I am saying here that when one has the authority of Jesus, every demon, angel, element, or whatever it may be has to obey. It has to kneel down and obey.

There is so much authority given to the believers. The word says;

**"At the name of Jesus every knee should bow..."**
**Philippians 2:10**

You see, the name was given as an authoritative signature we use. When that name is uttered by a believer, demons have to listen. The name was given as power of attorney.

The power of attorney is authorisation given to act on someone else's behalf in a legal or other matter. Believers have been authorised to act on the Lord Jesus' behalf. So when they call on the name of Jesus, it is as though the Lord Jesus Himself is the one doing the calling or commanding of things to happen. It is a very powerful thing.

Notice this person working on behalf of the grantor has the same power. A believer possesses the same authority as his grantor and demons know it.

Now, if one has authority, they should be having it to authorise something. See, authority itself, if it cannot execute, is nothing.

Think of the same policeman we spoke of, if he waves his hand to stop a vehicle and the vehicle does not stop, it does not indicate lack of authority on the policeman's part. It indicates that something else is missing. This policeman will have a badge, a gun, a uniform and all the things that will indicate he has power, but because authority is exercised in one way, the thing that should execute is another. So, there should be a link between the authority and the authoriser.

See, it is one thing for the policeman to signal a car to stop and another to physically stop it. Even if he is to raise his hand to stop it, he cannot force it physically because he might be run over. You see that?

If he is run over, the problem is not his authority, but his lack of physical strength to stop it. This is the same in the spiritual realm. The name of Jesus has authority, but it needs dunamis, kratos, and ishcus for one to start doing the job right. Dunamis is the force that effects a change, so it is needed in order to move things. However, dunamis also requires authority (exousia) for it to be legally used. When authority is there, there must be dunamis for this to begin to work.

There is therefore a relationship in dimensions in God's power needed, if anything is to work. There is an intertwining of these dimensions, if the believer is going to do anything right.

## Witnessing Authority At Work In My Church And Crusades

I have personally seen through my ministry people getting healed of different ailments. I remember one lady I ministered to who suffered from HIV Aids. The Lord told me to pick her out prophetically from a congregation I was ministering to. I whispered in her ear that God had told me she had this dreadful disease in her blood. She confirmed that it was true, and being a prophet, I have come to know that the Lord God only reveals a problem in order to solve it. Using the levels of power that I am teaching you right now, I spoke to that foul spirit and banished it from her body.

About a week later, the lady went to the hospital for a check up. To her amazement, she was ordered by her doctor to discontinue taking the numerous drugs she was taking, as her blood showed she was free from HIV AIDS.

It was gone, never to return again. Praise God!

This is a clear demonstration that when an intertwining of these dimensions takes place in your life, miracles can't help but show up in your life. Exousia also works better when this happens.

Kenneth Hagin, a father in the faith who made a big change in my life before his passing away was one of the men of God who had so much authority that even now many ministers call him their father. The Lord also told me about him being my spiritual father until his passing. Papa Hagin did not cease to be my father but by his passing God gave me someone who he says will be my mentor for life and both of these man were anointed with such authority that when you would get around them you would sense so much authority. So much exousia could be felt around them.

### Growing In Exousia

Exousia is increased in two main ways and these are; revelation and word. See here under revelation;

**"If any man is in Christ he is a new creature,** *behold***All things are become new..."**
**2 Cor. 5 vs. 17**

The word *BEHOLD* means "to see" or to "AWAKEN TO THE REALITY". So, one needs first to awaken to the fact that they are now new creatures in Christ, without that they will still sing songs of defeat and die of lack of knowledge. No wonder the Lord says;

**"My people perish for lack of knowledge..."**
**Hosea 4 vs. 6**

People die for the lack of knowledge. So knowledge, if it's nowhere to be found, will kill you. It will destroy you if you are not aware or have not awakened to the reality of who you are in Christ. Every believer needs awareness here. They need to understand that they are new in Christ. They have to know that they are God's sperm!

**"...born of incorruptible seed (sperma)..."**
**1 Peter 1 vs. 23**

That's what the word says. When one understands their royalty in Christ, they grow in exousia. It is a sure-fire way of growing in exousia. One needs a revelation, an opening of hidden things, an eye-opener so as to comprehend what it means to be a new creature in Christ Jesus.

A believer also has to be in the word a lot, so as to understand the extent of their power and the greatness of their ability.

1 Peter 2 vs. 2-3 says
**"Desire the sincere milk of the word..."**

So that what will happen?

**"...so that ye may grow by it..."**

God is not looking for spiritual babies to use. He is looking for those that have matured; those whose words are sure.

Criticism is not found near them, gossip is far away from them, and slander is banned from their mouths. He does not want a 25 year old man or 40 or 60 or more, who is still in a diaper sucking a pacifier.

God wants those who are willing to mature in the word and these are those who truly know who they are in Christ, because the word gave them light and illuminated their position in Christ that to them no demon can be superior. See!

**"... far above principalities, powers, dominion..."**
**Ephesians 1 vs. 21**

If one is a reader of the word they would know this scripture and know that the only way to get to authority is to have a base knowledge of where they are and who they are that would make them invincible. That is, above exousia, they have kratos too. See how it interlinks.

When the word is in you, exousia is in you because you bear fruit by the word. Study daily; spend hours in the word for the word says;

**"The entrance of thy word giveth light..."**
**Psalm 119 vs. 130**

It gives revelation that in turn makes you aware of the extent of your authority that when demons come, you know you are superior and they know you are superior too. It's very simple!

You bear fruit more when you are in the word and obey it. Notice these words from the master;

**"I am the true vine and my father the vinedresser, every branch in me that does not bear fruit HE TAKES AWAY" John 15 vs. 1,2.**

IF He takes away those with no fruit because they have no word and do not obey the word, then demons can take you out no matter how much you cry "Jesus!"

You will be counted among the "sons" of Sceva" if you do not back the exousia you have with dunamis and kratos, increased through the word. James 1 vs. 22 says;

**"...be a doer of the word..."**
**James 1 vs.22**

The word also has to be done; otherwise you will be wasting time. The word undone is potential unrecognised. No word, no power. No power, no exousia - no demon or circumstance listening or obeying.

Grow in exousia by growing in the word and in all your growing get revelation. Get understanding and act upon your understanding, which is imparted by God as you read the word.

## Understanding Is Vital

Revelation is very important. I remember one conference when I saw a man casting out demons. The whole thing was quite scary for the people who were there and I could not understand why he was struggling but then the Lord said it was revelation. He said the man had power to drive the demons out, but he had no revelation. Since this man was a person I knew, I told him and he argued saying I should try it myself. The chance came and immediately as I stood the demons literally left at high sprint.

They could not stand. There was too much revelation in me that they were pushed out. Don't get it wrong, I carried dunamis, but I also knew I had judicial precedence. This man had power, but he did not have revelation on his authority. For him, it was like having bullets but no gun. You just know it won't work!

How explosive is this source called Jesus! Can we see it once more?

**Colossians 1 vs. 14-19** answers this question;

**"...in whom we (you and I) have redemption through his blood, the forgiveness of sins. He is the image of the invisible God, the firstborn over all creation. For by him all things were created that are in heaven and that are on earth, visible and invisible, whether thrones or dominions or**

**principalities or powers. All things were created through Him and for Him and He is before all things andin Him all things consist and He is the head of the body, the church, who is the beginning, the firstborn from the dead, that in all things He may have pre-eminence. For it pleased the father that in Him all the fullness should dwell"**

Apostle Paul says here that Christ has pre-eminence and it pleased the father that all fullness dwells in him. So, this source is higher than any source, whether human or spirit; and when he calls, all should bow; and that same authority of Christ drives exousia.

Grow in it and see how it will work. Know it and grow in its revelation through the word and see yourself surprise your world.

## What You Don't Know Will Kill You

### "My people perish for lack of knowledge..." Hosea 4vs.6

Lack of knowledge on how exousia works or the extent of its power can harm your life. I remember when my wife and I were lecturers at this college. We had done well at the University of Salford in the United Kingdom. We both won the best student awards in our respective years; but though we were that good, we were just treated as foreigners who were lecturers. The benefits that British lecturers would get in their lives were not available to us, why? We were foreigners. This was not because of any bad practice at the college, but it is the practice in most countries; citizens will sometimes get priority. Different benefits are available for different people.

A time came when we naturalised and became citizens. We started enjoying those extra benefits and it was after a long while that we realised that we had missed out on yet more advantages of being British citizens. As far as we were concerned, we were partaking of *all* the benefits that come with being British citizens, when in actual fact, there was a whole lot more we missed out on. We were blinded, so we went without these great advantages.

See, we had all the evidence that proved our new citizenship (passports, certificates etc); but we did not know about so many other things, and we suffered due to ignorance. What you don't know can harm you!

There is a great need to know exousia, and how it can change your life; and when you get the extent of what you can do, then, use your rights and privileges in Christ.

Grow your exousia, give time to the word daily and to wisdom daily; get it, and in all your getting, get understanding, and you will see how explosive you will become.

### In Conclusion

There is a great interlink between the five dimensions of God's power that when you choose to grow in all of them as I have chosen to do as well, there is a transformation that will shock your world.

You need to understand that when you begin to move towards the top end realm of power, the devil will pull every punch through his kratos which is gossip, slander, criticism, and many other techniques; but when you see it happen, do not worry because that is the tonic of your anointing. It is the first proof you are moving higher.

Remember they said of Jesus;

### "...he deceiveth people..." John 7:12

People will talk and their talking should be a signature that you are causing a dent in the devils kingdom; otherwise they would have kept quiet. The devil only talks when you are doing something. So never listen to hearsay, criticism, and accusations. The Bible is clear on the source of accusation. It says the devil is the accuser of the brethren.

See, anyone who accuses someone Jesus Christ our Lord and saviour has died for, is being used of the devil, whether they know it or not. That is what the bible says. The word also says;

### "Woe (destruction) is unto you IF ALL MEN speak WELL OF YOU"
### Luke 6 vs. 26

The Lord's inspired word here says when ALL men speak well of you, then you are about to die. So, when you start moving in the exousia, dunamis, kratos, ischus, and even epikaizo, you become a dangerous person for the devil. The devil will not like it when you begin to be a man or woman of prayer, revelation, word, and character. He will not smile. He will send all he can.

### Summary Of Exousia

Notice, exousia refers to authority and grows by revelation and constant study of the word. It is literally hours of pouring the word into yourself and reading Christian material on authority and the power of the believer. Here, one wants to make sure they understand their position in Christ.

It is most essential. It is not only reading, but reading with understanding. That is, reading with apocalypses coming at the same time. Reading with a revelation being loaded into one's spirit until every pore on your body, every bone in you, every cell of your blood gets the message.

## Dunamis In Summary

Dunamis is power that explodes bullets. It is, as said before, a power plant of inherent power that gives authority or exousia something to exercise. It is the greatest partner to exousia, but used on its own cannot accomplish its desired outcome. This is developed through the word, but mostly through praying in the spirit; for then it can edify the spirit or build it up for it to sustain more power from on high. Notice;

"...if I pray in an unknown tongue, my spirit prays..."
**1 Cor. 14 vs. 14**

So, if Apostle Paul does not pray in tongues, he says his spirit will not pray. Do you see that? That is why we put 'if', that means the opposite is true. So the opposite would read;

**"If I do not pray in an unknown tongue my spirit will not pray...
(Opposite of the scripture above)"**

He also says;

**"He that prays in tongues edifies himself"**

This shows that praying in tongues builds oneself. He is saying 'I recharge' my batteries if I pray in tongues. In a nutshell, he is saying I increase in dunamis when I pray in tongues, so tongues are a major player in increasing dunamis.

## Kratos In Summary

Kratos is the power of invincibility. It is the power that brings immunity. It is the engine behind control. This is the highest power of God, just behind Epikaizo. Kratos, like any other dimension, has to work with all dimensions for it to go deep into great areas of effectiveness.

This is solely fed by the power of the spoken and written word. It is the stage of logos turning into rhema to effect a change. Kratos level gives immunity like what Apostle Paul said about the armour of God.

**"Put on the whole armour of God, that ye may be able to stand against the wiles of the devil"**
**Ephesians 6 vs. 11**

It grants divine cover from enemies; that is why the word says;

**"...wherewith ye shall be able to quench all the fiery darts**
**of the enemy" Ephesians 6 vs. 16.**

It offers protection, but cannot offer efficiency. Efficiency comes from another dimension.

## Ischus Summary

Ischus is the power of efficiency. It is the lubricating power of God that makes every other dimension work consistently. It gives lubrication to the working of all the dimensions and is increased by hours in prayer. It is hours in prayer that builds character. The main focus of ishcus is character built through prayer. Character is very necessary here. It is the main part here, but it's character built by prayer.

Ishcus is built when consistency in church attendance, giving, respecting those in ministry, loving everyone, being peaceful is achieved. In short, it is just a character responding power. It increases with character cultivated through prayer.

### Now;

...if you have seen soldiers in training, they are told to march every time when the commander shouts something which the soldiers pay attention to and follow immediately. What many do not know is that these soldiers are never told before the training where or when they are going to stop or where or when they are going to be instructed to turn in a certain direction. They are not told how many steps they have to march forward before they stop. They just follow the sound and they turn.

If the commander does not say anything, they will keep marching forward, why? It's because the command has not been given to stop or turn.

All this is done to create a mind that can follow strict orders in real battle situation. So, if they are told to fire, they do so without question. If told to stop, they will do it; for the training that looked like child's play, has created something great in them. It built their character – the marching helped them.

That is the same with developing character in the child of God. It teaches you how to obey the Lord; and prayers, as well as obedience, are the best ways for ishcus to lubricate every dimension. Ishcus is paramount. It may look like nothing much as compared to the other dimensions, but it is very important.

CHAPTER SIX

## The Big One: Epikaizo In Summary

Epikaizo is the boiling point of all power!

Epikaizo is the nearest to eternity. This is the power at the border of mortality and the beginning of immortality. Enoch had it and could not come back, because his power would have caused people to explode and so had Elijah. They had to be taken out of the earth to heaven. You also need to understand that Epikaizo like all other dimension comes as a result of God's sovereign rule and will. However God's will had principles and many of those principles are outlined in the word so we can search them out and make ourselves candidates to this Epikaizo level. Epikaizo makes one a superhuman!

Moses had it too, to the extent that God had to remind him to die! God came to Moses and told him;

**"...Get thee unto Mount Nebo..."**
**Deuteronomy 32: 49-50**

And Moses asked what he was supposed to do there up the mountain. He did not vocalise the question, but God knew he had it in his head, so he told him

**"AND DIE...! Verse 50a**

Wow, the man was too loaded now with epikaizo.

*Epikaizo* came upon Mary and the Lord was conceived. It came during the transfiguration and the disciples were blocked and fell down as dead. Epikaizo came upon Peter and his shadow healed the sick. He did not even have to lay hands on the sick people.

Epikaizo even fell on the handkerchiefs. The handkerchief felt nothing, smelt nothing but was able to heal the sick, all because of epikaizo. Just right here I need to encourage you like I was encouraged. Here it is – YOU ARE BETTER THAN A HANDKERCHIEF! If a handkerchief can receive epikaizo, you can!

This power like ishcus relies on prayer, but here, this is more than ischus. It is a higher dimension of prayer where one feels the burden of the load and goes for extensive hours, and many times, groans in the spirit until joy is produced. People who live in this dimension are loaded with power.

One of them was St Patricks who banished snakes from Ireland. He raised the dead and did many wonderful things.

He even prayed for an ugly man to look handsome.

The story goes that this man was too ugly so that the whole village laughed at him. He heard of St Patrick and went to him for help. St Patrick unnerved asked the man to identify the face he wanted to look like after prayer, and the man indicated that he wanted to look like the most handsome man known in that village. St Patricks sent for the handsome man and requested a blanket, which he used to cover the ugly man and the handsome man. He prayed right there in front of the villagers, and to everyone's surprise, the ugly man looked exactly like the handsome man, except for the height.

St Patrick asked the man if he wanted the same height, and he indicated that he wanted the same height; and it is known that after the second prayer, people could only tell them apart by their clothes. That is epikaizo in operation. Is it difficult to believe? That's because many believers are used to low dimensions of power or no power at all in many cases.

It is intimacy in prayer and constant stay in prayer. Not just the few minutes and you're done type of prayer; I am talking about hours and hours of groaning that will turn into joy in prayer.

Realise that it's possible to pray and not like the prayer time; that will not get you epikaizo. Epikaizo is enjoying time spent in prayer with the Lord, like what you are doing and love the one you are praying to. Understand how the Lord feels about you and other people. Feel His burden and you will be staring right into epikaizo.

Wigglesworth understood it. During His time he prayed to God and God told him His burden for souls. Wigglesworth vowed that he would win a soul per day, and that he did all his years; one soul per day, as the minimum. That was part of why he moved in epikaizo.

Many times people would run away and stand outside the church when Wigglesworth prayed, fearing for their lives because a cloud would fill the church. He was a man of epikaizo.

I remember in one of my crusades a demon manifested in one lady and the lady cried out in fear. She started running away from me in fear until I caught up with her. I asked her "why are you running away?"
she answered;"I am afraid"
I asked her "why?" and she said,
"I see the Lord Jesus Christ"
"Where do you see him?" I asked and she said,
"I see him all over you"

Now that is difficult to understand if you do not get

the revelation of the EPIKAIZO. What happened here was that the Lord Jesus Christ EPIKAIZOD ME to the extend where I was no longer visible to the demons. The demons where now seeing the Lord all over me. The demons where confused. Epikaizo had consumed my flesh and replaced it with the shining brightness of the Lord Jesus Christ that when I walked the demons saw the Lord Jesus Christ walking.

Epikaizo get you deep in the Lord. It transforms your relationship with God. You start to know the Lord INTIMATELY.

### Go Deep With The Lord

Make your prayers conversations with a lover called Jesus Christ. That is how it works. That is how it all comes to pass.

Make time with the Lord. Pray hours per day, even sixteen hours per day if you can. Spend the whole day with just him. Enjoy that presence and see what you will be like. You can surprise your people. The trick is not doing it religiously; it is in loving to do it. See this about epikaizo;

**"He that dwells in the secret place of the MOST HIGH, Shall abide under the shadow..."**
**Psalm 91 vs. 1**

There is the shadow again. The Epikaizo of the Most High, if one dwells there, ishcus the power of consistency and efficiency, is implied by the word 'dwells'.

The secret place means a place of intimate prayer where, when one stays permanently, he will be a powerful believer. In a nutshell, epikaizo is reached through spending time in prayer.

Kathryn + Esther + Mering

I remember asking the Lord for this level and the Lord took me in the Spirit back to the days of Wigglesworth, Maria Woodwerth Etter, and Karthryn Kuhlman. I saw them heal the sick and do mighty works. As I saw them, I cried again unto the Lord for this same working of power that could win millions to Christ; and what He said still rings in my ear today.

He said "Son, imagine yourself with a little deeper prayer." Epikaizo comes from a deep relationship with God; A deeper prayer life.

## Spending Time In Prayer

Watch how Apostle Paul does it, he says;

**"My little children in whom I labour or** *travail* **in birth..."**
**Galatians 4 vs. 19**

The word travail there is "***agonia***" and it refers to a deep emotion done while one is doing something. Here he is saying, "I agonia" for the Galatians. He is implying a contraction in prayer where he is deep in prayer. It is not just a two minute job. It is an agonia, but not with the Lord, but others and for you, for God's benefit.

When you do this, it surpasses the prayer for ischus. Here Apostle Paul was doing some deep prayer that is due to *agonia* happening, because he felt for the people and wanted them to walk in God. For epikaizo to take place, no pain, no gain, but don't get it wrong, this is not supposed to be ceremonial or religious. Deep intimacy with God will cause agonia in the spirit.

This is what the word says about the Spirit

**"...groaning..." Romans 8:26**

It is a level of birthing in prayer. The constructions in prayer that are too deep, they require mature people to see the spiritual sense. It is a higher level of prayer, far above the ischus dimension, but still builds the ischus too. Do you see the interlinking is back again?

You might even ask, what is the difference between this groaning in the Spirit and praying in tongues to increase dunamis? The difference is in the pace. You achieve faster in groaning in the spirit than praying in tongues. However, for you to groan, you should also have a spirit edified by tongues.

When that spirit is edified, one needs to have a revelation on what burden is placed upon them by God or others, or for something in order to start groaning. You don't start it; it just comes when one is aware of what God wants done.

CHAPTER SEVEN

## The Believer's Rights And Confessions

As a believer, you can recognise now that you have authority over demons and authority with God.

If you choose to grow in all these dimensions you can see, and will without fail see a great change in your circumstances. Nature will listen to you. Things that do not understand your language will listen to you.

I once spoke to a slug that had crawled in my house and within a short period it died before my eyes. I told it "if you move towards this door you will die at this point".
I made a mark and as it moved towards the mark, I looked to see it die; because I knew the authority I had, and as sure as I said it, it did not even cross that mark. It just died when its head hit the mark. It dried up as if it had been dead for a long time in that spot.

I have spoken to trees, tumours, and things that should not normally understand any language. Slugs do not speak English the last time I checked. So when I spoke to it, I spoke to its make-up and God made it understand and listen. The mark I put on the ground also knew if this thing disobeys, there is *dunamis* poured on it to kill it. It tried to disobey my exousia, but my dunamis and kratos grew and it was *epikaizoed* out of this earth. The dimensions killed it!

Pray, study the word, obey the word consistently, worship Him, build a Godly character, and have a revelation on a daily bases and the five dimensions of God's power will be for you.

You will surprise your world and win souls for God!

## Confessions:

Here are some scriptures you can start to meditate upon, as you prepare to move in the miraculous power of God:

- **"Behold, I give you the authority to trample on serpents and scorpions, and over all the power of the enemy, and nothing shall by any means hurt you." (Luke 10:19)**
- **"Then He called His twelve disciples together and gave them power and authority over all demons, and to cure diseases." (Luke 9:1)**
- **"And He called the twelve to Him, and began to send them out two by two, and gave them power over unclean spirits ... And they cast out many demons, and anointed with oil many who were sick, and healed them." (Mark 6: 7,13)**

- **"And when He had called His twelve disciples to Him, He gave them power over unclean spirits, to cast them out, and to heal all kinds of sickness and all kinds of disease." (Matthew 10:1)**

- **"But go rather to the lost sheep of the house of Israel. And as you go, preach, saying, 'The kingdom of heaven is at hand.' Heal the sick, cleanse the lepers, raise the dead,** cast out demons. Freely you have received, freely give." (Matthew 10:6)

- "No weapon formed against you shall prosper, and every tongue which rises against you in judgment you shall condemn. This is the heritage of the servants of the Lord, and their righteousness is from me," says the Lord. (Isaiah 54:17)

- "Through You we will push down our enemies; through Your name we will trample those who rise up against us. For I will not trust in my bow, nor shall my sword save me. But You have saved us from our enemies, and have put to shame those who hated us. In God we boast all day long, and praise Your name forever." (Psalm 44:5,6,7,8)

- "For the eyes of the Lord run to and fro throughout the whole earth, to show Himself strong on behalf of those whose heart is loyal to Him." (2 Chronicles 16:9)

- "... but the people who know their God shall be strong, and carry out great exploits." (Daniel 11:32)

- "This is the word of the Lord to Zerubbabel: 'Not by might, nor by power, but by My Spirit,' says the Lord of hosts. (Zechariah 4:6)

- "But you shall receive power when the Holy Spirit has come upon you; and you shall be witnesses to Me in Jerusalem, and in all Judea and Samaria, and to the end of the earth." (Acts 1:8)

- "For our gospel did not come to you in

word only, but also in power, and in the Holy Spirit ..." (1 Thessalonians 1:5)

- "For the kingdom of God is not in word but in power." (1 Corinthians 4:20)

- "... in mighty signs and wonders, by the power of the Spirit of God ..." (Romans 15:19)

- "Truly the signs of an apostle were accomplished among you with all perseverance, in signs and wonders and mighty deeds." (2 Corinthians 12:12)

- "God also bearing witness both with signs and wonders, with various miracles, and gifts of the Holy Spirit ..." (Hebrews 2:4)

- "And they went out and preached everywhere, the Lord working with them and confirming the word through the accompanying signs. Amen." (Mark 16:20)

- "And with great power the apostles gave witness to the resurrection of the Lord Jesus. And great grace was upon them all." (Acts 4:33)

- "But the anointing which you have received from Him abides in you ..." (1 John 2:27)

- "But you have an anointing from the Holy One, and you know all things." (1 John 2:20)

- "Then fear came upon every soul, and many wonders and signs were done through the apostles." (Acts 2:43)

- "No man shall be able to stand before

you all the days of your life; as I was with Moses, so I will be with you. I will not leave you nor forsake you. Be strong and of good courage ..." (Joshua 1:5)

- "Blessed be the Lord my Rock, who trains my hands for war, and my fingers for battle - my loving kindness and my fortress, my high tower and my deliverer, my shield and the One in whom I take refuge, who subdues my people under me." (Psalm 144:1)

- "For You are my lamp, O Lord; the Lord shall enlighten my darkness. For by You I can run against a troop; by my God I can leap over a wall. As for God, His way is perfect; the word of the Lord is proven; He is a shield to all who trust in Him." (2 Samuel 22:29)

- "It is God who arms me with strength, and makes my way perfect. He makes my feet like the feet of deer, and sets me on high places. He teaches my hands to make war, so that my arms can bend a bow of bronze ... I have pursued my enemies and overtaken them; neither did I turn back again till they were destroyed. I have wounded them, so that they were not able to rise; they have fallen under my feet. For You have armed me with strength for the battle; You have subdued under me those who rose up against me." (Psalm 18:32,37)

- I can do all things through Christ who strengthens me." (Philippians 4:13)

- "The Lord is my strength and my shield ..." (Psalm 28:7)

- "In the day when I cried out, you answered me, and made me bold with strength in my soul." (Psalm 138:3)

- "O God, You are more awesome than Your holy places. The God of Israel is He who gives strength and power to His people." (Psalm 68:35)

- "He gives power to the weak, and to those who have no might He increases strength." (Isaiah 40:29)

- "For the Lord will be your confidence, and will keep your foot from being caught." (Proverbs 3:26)

- "Yet the righteous will hold to his way, and he who has clean hands will be stronger and stronger." (Job 17:9)

- "They shall walk after the Lord. He will roar like a lion. When He roars, then His sons shall come trembling from the west ..." (Hosea 11:10)

- "If you faint in the day of adversity, your strength is small." (Proverbs 24:10)

- "Jesus answered and said unto them, You are mistaken, not knowing the scriptures, nor the power of God". (Matthew 22:29

- "Behold, I send the promise of My Father upon you: but tarry you in the city of Jerusalem, until you be endued with power from on high". (Luke 24:49)

- And Stephen, full of faith and power, did great wonders and miracles among the people. (Acts 6:8)

- How God anointed Jesus of Nazareth with the Holy Ghost and with power: Who went about doing good, and healing all that were oppressed of the devil; for God was with Him. (Acts 10:38)

- Then said Jesus to them again, Peace be unto you: as My Father hath sent Me, even so send I you.. And when He had said this, He breathed on them, and saith unto then, Receive you the Holy Ghost(John 20:21 -22)

-
- For I am not ashamed of the gospel of Jesus Christ: for it is the power of God unto salvation to everyone that believeth; to the Jew first, and also to the Greek. (Romans 1:16)

The Wait is OVER    pg 61 Good news
daily.   Dunamis - inherent power -
it was already    given to them.

CPSIA information can be obtained
at www.ICGtesting.com
Printed in the USA
BVHW042134221021
619670BV00008BA/45

9 780955 811692